3rd Workshop on Cognitive Modeling and Computational Linguistics 2012

(CMCL 2012)

Held at the 2012 Conference of the North American Chapter of the Association for Computational Linguistics: Human Language Technologies (NAACL-HLT 2012)

Montreal, Quebec, Canada
3-8 June 2012

ISBN: 978-1-62276-545-4

Printed from e-media with permission by:

Curran Associates, Inc.
57 Morehouse Lane
Red Hook, NY 12571

Some format issues inherent in the e-media version may also appear in this print version.

Printed by Curran Associates, Inc. (2013)

For permission requests, please contact the Association for Computational Linguistics at the address below.

Association for Computational Linguistics
209 N. Eighth Street
Stroudsburg, Pennsylvania 18360

Phone: 1-570-476-8006
Fax: 1-570-476-0860

acl@aclweb.org

Additional copies of this publication are available from:

Curran Associates, Inc.
57 Morehouse Lane
Red Hook, NY 12571 USA
Phone: 845-758-0400
Fax: 845-758-2634
Email: curran@proceedings.com
Web: www.proceedings.com

Introduction

The 2012 Workshop on Cognitive Modeling and Computational Linguistics is the third workshop in this series and stands in the tradition of a number of related workshops that apply computational modeling to questions of cognitive, linguistic nature: the workshop on Psychocomputational Models of Human Language Acquisition, the Workshop on Production of Referring Expressions, or the Incremental Parsing workshop (ACL 2004). In short, CMCL aims to provide a venue for high-quality work in computational psycholinguistics.

This year, we have received 22 submissions and accepted 10 after careful review. One of those has been withdrawn. We thank all submitting authors as well as the dedicated program committee for making this happen.

Roger Levy and David Reitter

Organizers:

Roger Levy, University of California, San Diego
David Reitter, Carnegie Mellon University and Penn State University

Program Committee:

Klinton Bicknell (UC San Diego)
Matthew Crocker (Saarbrücken University)
Robert Daland (UC Los Angeles)
Vera Demberg (Saarbrücken University)
Brian Dillon (University of Massachussetts)
Amit Dubey (University of Edinburgh)
Naomi Feldman (University of Maryland)
Michael C. Frank (Stanford University)
Noah Goodman (Stanford University)
Peter beim Graben (Humboldt University Berlin)
John T. Hale (Cornell University)
Keith Hall (Google)
Jeffrey Heinz (University of Delaware)
T. Florian Jaeger (University of Rochester)
Gaja Jarosz (Yale University)
Frank Keller (University of Edinburgh)
Lars Konieczny (University of Freiburg)
Richard L. Lewis (University of Michigan)
Brian Edmond Murphy (University of Trento)
Lisa Pearl (UC Irvine)
Ulrike Padó (VICO Research & Consulting)
Sebastian Padó (University of Heidelberg)
Amy Perfors (Adelaide University)
Brian Roark (Oregon Health & Science University)
William Schuler (The Ohio State University)
Nathaniel Smith (UC San Diego)
Mark Steedman (University of Edinburgh)
Patrick Sturt (University of Edinburgh)
Shravan Vasishth (University of Potsdam)
Guodong Zhou (Soochow University)

Table of Contents

Workshop Program

(9:30 AM) Acquisition and Representation

Modeling the Acquisition of Mental State Verbs
Libby Barak, Afsaneh Fazly and Suzanne Stevenson

Semi-supervised learning for automatic conceptual property extraction
Colin Kelly, Barry Devereux and Anna Korhonen

(11:30 AM) Structure and Processing I

Why long words take longer to read: the role of uncertainty about word length
Klinton Bicknell and Roger Levy

Minimal Dependency Length in Realization Ranking
Michael White and Rajakrishnan Rajkumar

(2 PM) Structure and Processing II

Fractal Unfolding: A Metamorphic Approach to Learning to Parse Recursive Structure
Whitney Tabor, Pyeong Whan Cho and Emily Szkudlarek

Connectionist-Inspired Incremental PCFG Parsing
Marten van Schijndel, Andy Exley and William Schuler

Sequential vs. Hierarchical Syntactic Models of Human Incremental Sentence Processing
Victoria Fossum and Roger Levy

(4 PM) Memory

Modeling covert event retrieval in logical metonymy: probabilistic and distributional accounts
Alessandra Zarcone, Jason Utt and Sebastian Padó

A Computational Model of Memory, Attention, and Word Learning
Aida Nematzadeh, Afsaneh Fazly and Suzanne Stevenson

Modeling the Acquisition of Mental State Verbs

Libby Barak, Afsaneh Fazly, and **Suzanne Stevenson**
Department of Computer Science
University of Toronto
Toronto, Canada
{libbyb,afsaneh,suzanne}@cs.toronto.edu

Abstract

Children acquire mental state verbs (MSVs) much later than other, lower-frequency, words. One factor proposed to contribute to this delay is that children must learn various semantic and syntactic cues that draw attention to the difficult-to-observe mental content of a scene. We develop a novel computational approach that enables us to explore the role of such cues, and show that our model can replicate aspects of the developmental trajectory of MSV acquisition.

1 Introduction

Mental State Verbs (MSVs), such as *think*, *know*, and *want*, are very frequent in child-directed language, yet children use them productively much later than lower-frequency action verbs, such as *fall* and *throw* (Johnson and Wellman, 1980; Shatz et al., 1983). Psycholinguistic theories have suggested that there is a delay in the acquisition of MSVs because they require certain cognitive and/or linguistic skills that are not available during the early stages of language development. For example, MSVs typically occur with a sentential complement (SC) that refers to the propositional content of the mental state, as in *He thinks Mom went home*. Children have to reach a stage of syntactic development that includes some facility with SCs in order to fully acquire MSVs. However, even at 3–5 years old, children are able to process SCs only imperfectly (e.g., Asplin, 2002).

Even when children are able to produce SCs with other verbs (such as verbs of communication, as in *He said Mom went home*), there is a lag before they productively use MSVs referring to actual mental content (Diessel and Tomasello, 2001).[1] Psycholinguists have suggested that young children lack the conceptual ability to conceive that others have mental states separate from their own (Bartsch and Wellman, 1995; Gopnik and Meltzoff, 1997), further delaying the acquisition of MSVs.

Another factor suggested to contribute to the difficulty of acquiring MSVs is their *informational requirements* (Gleitman et al., 2005; Papafragou et al., 2007). Children learn word meanings by figuring out which aspects of an observed scene are referred to by a particular word (Quine, 1960). MSVs often refer to aspects of the world that are not directly observable (i.e., the beliefs and desires of another entity). Thus, in addition to the above-mentioned challenges posed by children's developing linguistic/conceptual abilities, children may simply have difficulty in identifying the relevant mental content necessary to learning MSVs.

In particular, Papafragou et al. (2007) [PCG] have shown that even given adequate conceptual and linguistic abilities (as in adults) the mental events in a scene (the actors' internal states) are not attended to as much as the actions, unless there are cues that heighten the salience of the mental content. PCG further demonstrate that children's sensitivity to such cues lags behind that of adults, suggesting an additional factor in the acquisition of MSVs which

[1] Researchers have noted that children use MSVs in fixed phrases, in a performative use or as a pragmatic marker, well before they use them to refer to actual mental content (e.g., Diessel and Tomasello, 2001; Shatz et al., 1983). Here by "acquisition of MSVs", we are specifically referring to children learning usages that genuinely refer to mental content.

is the developmental change in how strongly such cues are associated with the relevant mental content.

We develop a computational model of MSV acquisition (the first, to our knowledge) to further illuminate these issues. We extend an existing model of verb argument structure acquisition (Alishahi and Stevenson, 2008) to enable the representation and processing of mental state semantics and syntax. We simulate the developmental change proposed by PCG through a gradually increasing ability in the model to appropriately attend to the mental content of a scene. In addition, we suggest that even when the learner's *semantic* representation is biased towards the action content, the learner attends to the observed SC *syntax* in an MSV utterance. This is especially important to account for the pattern of errors in child data. Our model thus extends the account of PCG to show that a probabilistic interplay of the semantic and syntactic features of a partial and somewhat erroneous perception of the input, combined with a growing ability to attend to cues indicative of mental content, can help to account for children's developmental trajectory in learning MSVs.

2 Background and Our Approach

To investigate the linguistic and contextual cues that could help in learning MSVs, PCG use a procedure called the Human Simulation Paradigm (originally proposed by Gillette et al., 1999). In this paradigm, subjects are put in situations intended to simulate various word learning conditions of young children. E.g., in one condition, adults watch silent videos of caregivers interacting with children, and are asked to predict the verb uttered by the caregiver. In another condition, subjects hear a sentence containing a nonce verb (e.g., *gorp*) after watching the video, and are asked what *gorp* might mean.

We focus on two factors investigated by PCG in the performance of adults and children in identifying MSVs. The first factor they investigated involved the syntactic frame used when subjects were given a sentence with a nonce verb. PCG hypothesized that an SC frame would be a cue to mental content (and an MSV), since the SC refers to propositional content. The second factor PCG examined was whether the video described a "true belief" or a "false belief" scene: A true belief scene shows an ordinary situation which unfolds as the character in the scene expects — e.g., a little boy takes food to his grandmother, and she is there in the house as expected. The corresponding false belief scene has an unexpected outcome for the character — in this case, another character has replaced the grandmother in her bed. Here the hypothesis was that such false belief scenes would heighten the salience of mental activity in the scene and lead to greater belief verb responses in describing them.

PCG's results showed that both adults and children were sensitive to both the scene and syntax cues, but children's ability to draw on such cues was inferior to that of adults. They thus propose that the difference between children and adults is that children have not yet formed as strong an association as adults between the cues and the mental content of a scene as required to match the performance of adults. Nonetheless, their results suggest that the participating children had the conceptual and linguistic abilities required for MSVs, since they were able to produce them under conditions with sufficiently strong cues.

We simulate PCG's experiments using a novel computational approach. Following PCG, we assume that even when a learner is able to perceive the general semantic and syntactic properties of a belief scene and associated utterance, they may not attend to the mental content in every situation, and that this ability improves over time. We model a developmental change in a learner's attention to mental content: At early stages, corresponding to the state of young children, the learner largely focuses on the action aspects of a belief scene, even in the presence of an utterance using an MSV. Over time, the learner gradually increases in the ability to attend appropriately to the mental aspects of such a scene and utterance, until adult-like competence is achieved in associating the available cues with mental content.

Importantly, our work extends the proposal of PCG by bringing in evidence from other relevant studies on children's ability to process SCs. More specifically, we suggest that when children hear a sentence like *I think Mom went home*, they recognize (and record) the existence of an SC, while *at the same time* they focus on the action semantics as the main (most salient) event. In other words, we assume that children's imperfect syntactic abilities are at least sufficient to recognize the SC usage (Nelson et al., 1989; Asplin, 2002). However, their attention is mostly directed towards the action expressed in the embedded complement, either because mental content is less easily observable than action (Papafragou et al., 2007), or due to the linguistic saliency of the embedded clause (Diessel and Tomasello, 2001; Dehe and Wichmann, 2010). As mentioned above, we model this misrepresentation by considering the possibility of not attending to mental content in a belief scene. Specifically, we assume that (i) the model is very likely to overlook the mental content at earlier stages (corresponding to children's observed behaviour); and (ii) as the model 'ages' (i.e., receives more input), its attentional abilities improve and thus the model is more likely to focus on the mental content as the main proposition. Our results suggest that these changes to the model lead to a match between our model's behaviour and PCG's differential results for children and adults.

3 The Computational Model

A number of computational models have examined the role of interacting syntactic and semantic cues in the acquisition of verb argument structure (e.g., Niyogi, 2002; Buttery, 2006; Alishahi and Stevenson, 2008; Perfors et al., 2010; Parisien and Stevenson, 2011). However, to our knowledge no computational model has addressed the developmental trajectory in the acquisition of MSVs. Here we extend the verb argument structure acquisition model of Alishahi and Stevenson (2008) to enable it to account for MSV acquisition. Specifically, we use their core Bayesian learning algorithm, but modify the input processing component to reflect a developmental change in attention to the mental state content of an MSV usage and its consequent representation, as noted above.

We use this model for the following reasons: (i) it focuses on argument structure learning, and the interplay between syntax and semantics, which are key to MSV acquisition; (ii) it is probabilistic and hence can naturally capture gradient responses to different cues; and (iii) it is incremental, which allows us to investigate changes in behaviour over time. We first give an overview of the original model, and then explain our extensions.

3.1 Model Overview

The input to the model is a sequence of utterances (what the child hears), each paired with a scene (what the child perceives); see Table 1 for an example. First, the *frame extraction component* of the model extracts from the input pair a *frame*—a collection of *features*. We use features that include both semantic properties ('event primitives' and 'event participants') and syntactic properties ('syntactic pattern' and 'verb count'). See Table 2 for examples of two possible frames extracted from the pair in Table 1. Second, the *learning component* of the model incrementally clusters the extracted frames one by one. These clusters correspond to *constructions* that reflect probabilistic associations of semantic and syntactic features across similar usages, such as an agentive intransitive or causative transitive. The model can use these associations to simulate various language tasks as the prediction of a missing feature given others. For example, to simulate the human simulation paradigm setting, we can use the model to predict a missing verb on the basis of the available semantic and syntactic information (as in Alishahi and Pyykkoñen, 2011).

3.2 Algorithm for Learning Constructions

The model clusters the input frames into constructions on the basis of their overall similarity in the values of their features. Importantly, the model learns these constructions incrementally, considering the possibility of creating a new construction for a given frame if the frame is not sufficiently similar to any of the existing constructions. Formally, the model finds the best construction (including a new one) for a given frame F as in:

$$\text{BestConstruction}(F) = \underset{k \in Constructions}{\text{argmax}} \; P(k|F) \tag{1}$$

where k ranges over all existing constructions and a new one. Using Bayes rule:

$$P(k|F) = \frac{P(k)P(F|k)}{P(F)} \propto P(k)P(F|k) \tag{2}$$

The prior probability of each construction $P(k)$ is estimated as the proportion of observed frames that are in k, assigning a higher prior to constructions

$\text{Think}_{[state,consider,cogitate]}(\text{I}_{[experiencer,preceiver,considerer]},\text{Go}_{[physical,act,move]}(\text{MOM}_{[agent,actor,change]},\text{HOME}_{[location,destination]}))$ *I think Mom went home.*

Table 1: A sample Scene–Utterance input pair.

(a) Interpretation#1 (mental event is attended to)

main predicate	**think**
other predicate	go
event primitives	$\{$ *state, consider, cogitate* $\}$
event participants	$\{$ *experiencer, perceiver, considerer* $\}$ $\{$ *preposition, action, perceivable* $\}$
syntactic pattern	arg1 *verb* arg-S
verb count	2

(b) Interpretation#2 (mental event not attended to)

main predicate	**go**
other predicate	think
event primitives	$\{$ *physical, act, move* $\}$
event participants	$\{$ *agent, actor, change* $\}$ $\{$ *location, destination* $\}$
syntactic pattern	arg1 *verb* arg-S
verb count	2

Table 2: Two frames extracted from the scene–utterance pair in Table 1. The bottom left and right panels of the table describe the two possible interpretations given the input pair. (a) Interpretation#1 assumes that the mental event is the focus of attention. Here **think** is interpreted as the main predicate, which the event primitives and participants refer to. (b) Interpretation#2 assumes that attention is mostly directed to the physical action in the scene, and thus **go** is taken to be the main predicate, which also determines the extracted event primitives and participants. Note that for both interpretations, the learner is assumed to perceive the utterance in full, thus both verbs are heard in the context of the sentential complement syntax (i.e., syntactic pattern with SC and 2 verbs), without fully extracting the syntactic relations between the clauses.

that are more entrenched (i.e., observed more frequently). The likelihood $P(F|k)$ is estimated based on the values of features in F and the frames in k:

$$P(F|k) = \prod_{i \in frameFeatures} P_i(j|k) \qquad (3)$$

where i refers to the ith feature of F and j refers to its value. The conditional probability of a feature i to have the value j in construction k, $P_i(j|k)$, is calculated with a smoothed version of:

$$P_i(j|k) = \frac{\text{count}_i(j,k)}{n_k} \qquad (4)$$

where $\text{count}_i(j,k)$ reflects the number of times feature i has the value j in construction k, and n_k is the number of frames in k. We have two types of features: single-valued and set-valued. The result of the count_i operator for a single-valued feature is based on exact match to the value j, while the result for a set-valued feature is based on the degree of overlap between the compared sets, as in the original model.

3.3 Modeling Developmental Changes in Attending to Mental Content

We extend the model above to account for the increase in the ability to attend to cues associated with MSVs, as observed by PCG. In addition, we propose that children's representation of this situation includes the observed syntax of the MSV. That is, children do not simply ignore the MSV usage, focusing only on the action expressed in its complement — they must also note that this action semantics occurs in the context of an SC usage.

To adapt the model in these ways, we change the frame extraction component to allow two possible interpretations for a mental event input. First, to reflect PCG's proposal, we incorporate a mechanism into the model's frame-extraction process that takes into account the probability of attending to mental content. Specifically, we assume that when presented with an input pair containing an MSV, as in Table 1, a learner attends to the perceptually salient action/state expressed in the complement (here Go) with probability p, and to the non-perceptually salient mental event expressed in the main verb (here Think) with probability $1 - p$. This probability p is a function over time, corresponding to the observed developmental progression. At very early stages, p will be high (close to 1), simulating the much greater saliency of physical actions compared to mental events for younger children. With subsequent input, p will decrease, giving more and more attention to the mental content of a scene with a mental event, gradually approaching adult-like abilities.

We adopt the following function for p:

$$p = \frac{1}{\delta \cdot t + 1}, \quad 0 < \delta \ll 1 \qquad (5)$$

where t is the current time, expressed as the total number of scene–utterance pairs observed thus far by the model, and the parameter δ is set to a small value to assign a high probability to the physical action interpretation of the scene in the initial stages of learning (when t is small).

We must specify the precise make-up of the frames that correspond to the two possible interpretations considered with probability p and $1 - p$. PCG state only that children and adults differentially attend to the action vs. mental content of the scene. We operationalize this by forming two possible frames in response to an MSV usage. We propose that one of the frames (with probability $1-p$) is the interpretation of the mental content usage, as in Table 2(a). However, we extend the account of PCG by proposing that the other frame considered is not simply a standard representation of an action scene–utterance pair. Rather, we suggest that the interpretation of an MSV scene–utterance pair that focuses on the action semantics does so *within the context of the SC syntax*, given the assumed stage of linguistic abilities of the learner. This leads to the frame (with probability p) as in Table 2(b), which represents the action semantics within a two-verb construction associated with the SC syntax.

4 Experimental Setup

4.1 Input Data

We generate artificial corpora for our simulations, since we do not have access to sufficient data of actual utterances paired with scene representations. In order to create naturalistic data that resembles what children are exposed to, we follow the approach of Alishahi and Stevenson (2008) to build an input-generation lexicon that has the distributional properties of actual child-directed speech (CDS). Their original lexicon contains only high-frequency physical action verbs that appear in limited syntactic patterns. Our expanded lexicon also includes mental state, perception, and communication verbs, all of which can appear with SCs.

We extracted our verbs and their distributional properties from the child-directed speech of 8 children in the CHILDES database (MacWhinney, 2000).[2] We selected 28 verbs from different semantic classes and different frequency ranges: 12 physical action verbs taken from the original model (*come, go, fall, eat, play, get, give, take, make, look, put, sit*), 6 perception and communication verbs (*see, hear, watch, say, tell, ask*), 5 belief verbs (*think, know, guess, bet, believe*), and 5 desire verbs (*want, wish, like, mind, need*). For each verb, we manually analyzed a random sample of 100 CDS usages (or all usages if fewer than 100) to extract distributional information about its argument structures.

We construct the input-generation lexicon by listing each of the 28 verbs (i.e. the 'main predicate'), along with its overall frequency, as well as the frequency with which it appears with each argument structure. Each entry contains values of the syntactic and semantic features (see Table 2 for examples), including 'event primitives', 'event participants', 'syntactic pattern', and 'verb count'. By including these features, we assume that a learner is capable of understanding basic syntactic properties of an utterance, including word syntactic categories (e.g., noun and verb), word order, and the appearance of SCs (e.g., Nelson et al., 1989). We also assume that a learner has the ability to perceive and conceptualize the general semantic properties of events — including mental, perceptual, communicative, and physical actions — as well as those of the event participants. Values for the semantic features (the event primitives and event participants) are taken from Alishahi and Stevenson (2008) for the action verbs, and from several sources including VerbNet (Kipper et al., 2008) and Dowty (1991) for the additional verbs.

For each simulation in our experiments (explained below), we use the input-generation lexicon to automatically generate an input corpus of scene–utterance pairs that reflects the observed frequency distribution in CDS.[3] For an input utterance that contains an MSV, we randomly pick one of the action verbs as the verb appearing within the sentential complement (the 'other predicate').

[2] Corpora of Brown (1973); Suppes (1974); Kuczaj (1977); Bloom et al. (1974); Sachs (1983); Lieven et al. (2009).

[3] The model does not use the input-generation lexicon in learning.

4.2 Setup of Simulations

We perform simulations by training the model on a randomly generated input corpus, and examining changes in its performance over time with periodic tests. Specifically, we perform simulations of the verb identification task in the human simulation paradigm as follows: At each test point, we present the model with a *partial test frame* with missing predicate (verb) values, and different amounts of information for the other features. The tests correspond to the scenarios in the original experiments of PCG, where each scenario is represented by a partial frame as follows:

1. **scene-only scenario**: Corresponds to subjects watching a silent video depicting either an Action or a Belief scene. Our test frame includes values for the semantic features (event primitives and event participants) corresponding to the scene type, but no syntactic features.

2. **syntax-only scenario**: Corresponds to subjects hearing either an SC or a non-SC utterance. The test frame includes the corresponding syntactic pattern and verb count of the utterance type heard, but no semantic features.

3. **syntax & scene scenario**: Corresponds to subjects watching a silent video (with Action or Belief content), and hearing an associated (non-SC or SC) utterance. The test frame includes all the relevant syntactic and semantic features.

We perform 100 simulations, each on 15000 randomly-generated training frames, and examine the type of verbs that the model predicts in response to test frames for the three scenarios. For each scenario and each simulation, we generate a test frame by including the relevant feature values of a randomly-selected physical action or belief verb usage from the input-generation lexicon.

PCG code the individual verb responses of their human subjects into various verb classes. To analogously code our model's response to each test frame, we estimate the likelihood of each of two verb groups, Belief and Action,[4] by summing over the likelihood of all the verbs in that group. In the results below, these likelihood scores are averaged for each test point over the 100 simulations.

[4]The Action verbs include action, communication, and perception verbs, as in PCG. Verbs from the desire group are not considered here, also as in PCG.

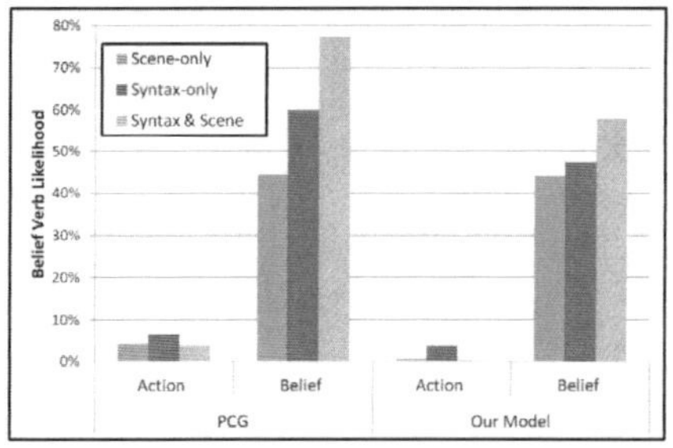

Figure 1: Likelihood of Belief verb prediction given Action or Belief input.

When our model is presented with a test frame containing a Belief scene, we assume that the model (like a language learner) may not attend to the mental content, resulting in one of the two interpretations described in Section 3.3 (see Table 2). We thus calculate the verb class likelihoods using a weighted average of the verbs predicted under the two interpretations. Following PCG, we test our model with two types of Belief scenes: True Belief and False Belief, with the latter having a higher level of belief saliency. We model the difference between these two scene types as a difference in the probabilities of perceiving the two interpretations, with a higher probability for the belief interpretation given a False Belief test frame. In the experiments presented here, we set this probability to 80% for False Belief, and to 60% (just above chance) for True Belief. (Unlike in training, where we assume a change over time in the probability of a belief interpretation, for each presentation of the test frame we use the same probabilities of the two interpretations.)

5 Experimental Results

We present two sets of results: In Section 5.1, we examine the role of syntactic and semantic cues in MSV identification, by comparing the likelihoods of the model's Belief verb predictions across the three scenarios. Here we test the model after processing 15000 input frames, simulating an adult-like behaviour (as in PCG). At this stage, we present the model with an Action test frame (Action scene and/or Transitive syntax), or a Belief test frame

(False Belief scene and/or SC syntax). In Section 5.2, we look into the role of semantic cues that enhance belief saliency, by comparing the likelihoods of Belief vs. Action verb predictions in the syntax & scene scenario. The test frames depict either a True Belief or a False Belief scene, paired with an SC utterance. Here, we test our model periodically to examine the developmental pattern of MSV identification, comparing our results with the difference in the behaviour of children and adults in PCG.

5.1 Linguistic Cues for Belief Verb Prediction

The left side of Figure 1 presents the results of PCG (for adult subjects); the right side shows the likelihood of Belief verb prediction by our model. Similar to the results of PCG, our model's likelihood of Belief verb prediction is extremely low when given an Action test frame (Action scene and/or Transitive syntax), whereas it is much higher when the model is presented with a Belief test frame (False Belief scene and/or SC syntax). Moreover, as in PCG, when the model is tested with Belief content, the lowest likelihood is for the scene-only scenario and the highest is for the syntax & scene scenario.

PCG found, somewhat surprisingly, that the syntax-only scenario was more informative for MSV prediction than the scene-only scenario. Our results replicate this finding, which we believe is due to the way our Bayesian clustering groups verb usages together. Non-SC usages of MSVs are often grouped with action verbs that frequently appear with non-SC syntax, and this results in constructions with mixed (action and belief) semantics. When using MSV semantic features to make the verb prediction, the action verbs get a higher likelihood based on such mixed constructions. However, the frequent usage of MSVs with SC results in entrenched constructions of mostly MSVs. Although other verbs, such as *see* and *say*, may also be used with SC syntax, they are grouped with verbs such as *watch* and *tell* into constructions with mixed (SC and non-SC) syntax. When given SC syntax in verb prediction, the more coherent MSV constructions result in a high likelihood of predicting Belief verbs.

5.2 Belief Saliency in Verb Prediction

Figure 2(a) shows the PCG results, for children and adults, and for True Belief and False Belief.

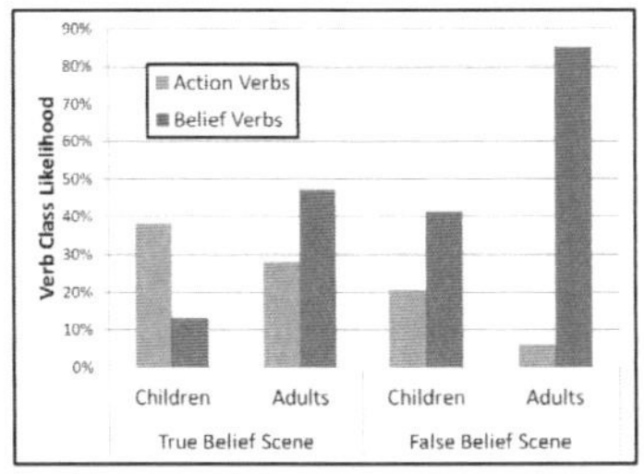

(a)

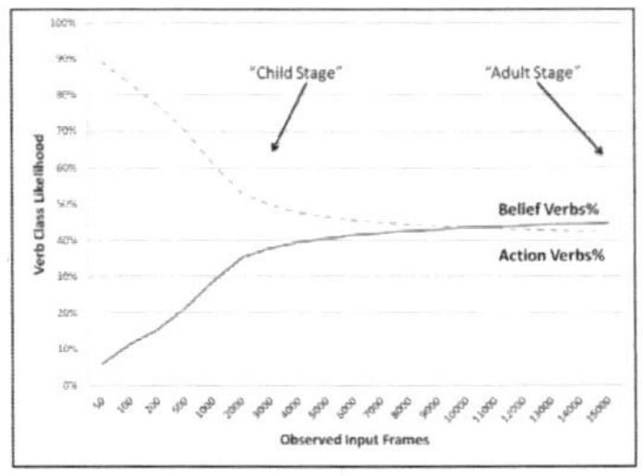

(b)

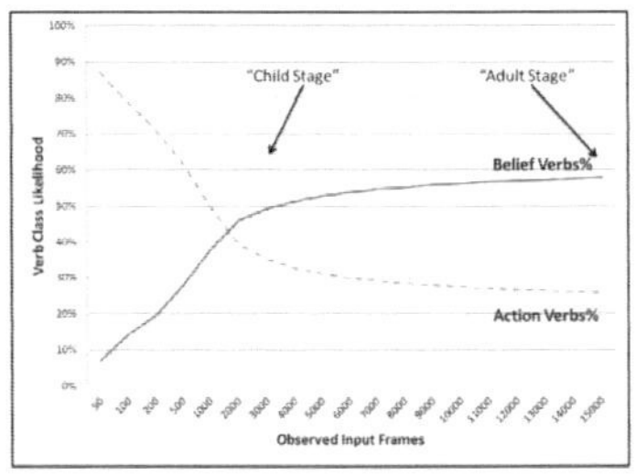

(c)

Figure 2: Verb class likelihood: (a) PCG results for adults and children (aged 3;7–5;9); (b) Model's results given True Belief; (c) Model's results given False Belief.

Figures 2(b) and (c) present the likelihoods of the model's Belief vs. Action verb prediction, over time, for True and False Belief situations (True/False Belief scene and SC syntax), respectively. We first compare the responses of our model at the final stage of training to those of adults in PCG. At this stage, the model's verb predictions (for both True and False Belief) follow a similar trend to that of adult subjects in PCG. The likelihood of Belief verbs is much higher than the likelihood of Action verbs given a False Belief situation. Moreover, the likelihood of Belief verbs is higher given a False Belief situation, compared to a True Belief situation.

Next, we compare the developmental pattern of Belief/Action verb predictions in the model with the difference in behaviour of children and adults in PCG. We focus on the model's responses after processing about 3000 input pairs, as it corresponds to the trends observed for the children in PCG. At this stage, the likelihood of Belief verbs is lower than that of Action verbs for the True Belief situation, but the pattern is reversed for False Belief; a pattern similar to children's behaviour in PCG (see Figure 2(a)). As in PCG, the likelihood of Belief verb predictions in our model is higher than that of Action verbs for the False Belief situation, in both "child" and "adult" stages, with a larger difference as the model 'ages' (i.e., processes more input). For the True Belief situation also the pattern is similar to that of PCG: Belief verbs are less likely than Action verbs to be predicted at early stages, but as the model receives more input, the likelihood of Belief verbs becomes slightly higher than that of Action verbs.

PCG's hypothesis of greater attention to the action content of a scene implicitly implies that children focus on the action semantics and syntax of the embedded SC of a Belief verb. We have suggested instead that the focus is on the action semantics within the context of the SC syntax of the MSV. To directly evaluate the necessity of our latter assumption, we performed a simulation using both action syntax and semantics to represent the physical interpretation of the belief scene. Specifically, the syntactic features in this representation were non-SC structure with only one verb. Based on these settings, the model predicted high likelihood for the Belief verbs from a very early stage, not showing the same delayed acquisition pattern exhibited by PCG's results. This result suggests that the SC syntax plays an important role in MSV acquisition.

6 Discussion

Various studies have considered why mental state verbs (MSVs) appear relatively late in children's productions (e.g., Shatz et al., 1983; Bartsch and Wellman, 1995). The Human Simulation Paradigm has revealed that adult participants tend to focus on the physical action cues of a scene (Gleitman et al., 2005). PCG's results further show that cues emphasizing mental content lead to a significant increase in MSV responses in such tasks. Moreover, they show that a sentential complement (SC) structure is a stronger cue to an MSV than the semantic cues emphasizing mental content.

In this paper we adapt a computational Bayesian model to analyze such semantic and syntactic cues in the ability of children to identify them. We simulate an attentional mechanism of the growing sensitivity to mental content in a scene into the model. We show that both the ability to observe the obscure mental content and the ability to recognize the use of an SC structure are essential to replicate PCG's observations. Moreover, our results predict the strong association of MSVs to the SC syntax, for the first time (to our knowledge) in a computational model.

Children often use verbs other than MSVs in experimental settings in which MSVs would be the appropriate or correct verb choice (Asplin, 2002; Kidd et al., 2006; Papafragou et al., 2007). Our model presents similar variability in verb choice. One underlying cause of this behaviour in the model is its association of action semantics to SC syntax, due to the tendency to observe the physical cues in a scene associated with an utterance using an MSV with an SC. Preliminary results (not reported here) imply that the association of perception and communication verbs that frequently appear with SC contribute to this pattern of verb choice (see de Villiers, 2005, for theoretical support). Our results require further work to fully understand this behaviour.

Finally, our model will facilitate future work in regards to the *performative usage* of MSVs, in which MSVs do not indicate mental content, but rather direct the conversation. Several studies (e.g., Diessel and Tomasello, 2001; Howard et al., 2008), have referred to the role performative use likely plays in MSV acquisition, since the first MSV usages by children are performative. The semantic properties MSVs take in performative usages is not currently represented in our lexicon. However, the physical interpretation of the mental scene that we have used in our experiments here is similar to the performative usage: i.e., the main perceived action and the observed syntactic structure are the same. At the moment, our results imply that the association of MSVs with their genuine mental meaning is delayed by interpretations of the mental scene which overlook the mental content. In the future, we aim to incorporate the semantic representation of performative usages to better analyze their effect on MSV acquisition.

References

Afra Alishahi and Pirita Pyykkoñen. 2011. The onset of syntactic bootstrapping in word learning: Evidence from a computational study. In *Proceedings of the 33st Annual Conference of the Cognitive Science Society*.

Afra Alishahi and Suzanne Stevenson. 2008. A computational model of early argument structure acquisition. *Cognitive Science*, 32(5):789–834.

Kristen N. Asplin. 2002. *Can complement frames help children learn the meaning of abstract verbs?* Ph.D. thesis, UMass Amherst.

Karen Bartsch and Henry M. Wellman. 1995. Children talk about the mind.

Lois Bloom, Lois Hood, and Patsy Lightbown. 1974. Imitation in language development: If, when, and why. *Cognitive Psychology*, 6(3):380–420.

Roger Brown. 1973. *A first language: The early stages*. Harvard U. Press.

Paula J. Buttery. 2006. Computational models for first language acquisition. Technical Report UCAM-CL-TR-675, University of Cambridge, Computer Laboratory.

Jill G. de Villiers. 2005. Can language acquisition give children a point of view. In *Why Language Matters for Theory of Mind*, pages 199–232. Oxford University Press.

Nicole Dehe and Anne Wichmann. 2010. Sentence-initial I *think (that)* and *i believe (that)*: Prosodic evidence for use as main clause, comment clause and dicourse marker. *Stuides in Language*, 34(1):36–74.

Holger Diessel and Michael Tomasello. 2001. The acquisition of finite complement clauses in english: A corpus-based analysis. *Cognitive Linguistics*, 12(2):97–142.

David Dowty. 1991. Thematic Proto-Roles and Argument Selection. *Language*, 67(3):547–619.

Jane Gillette, Lila Gleitman, Henry Gleitman, and Anne Lederer. 1999. Human simulations of lexical acquisition. *Cognition*, 73(2):135–176.

Lila R. Gleitman, Kimberly Cassidy, Rebecca Nappa, Anna Papafragou, and John C. Trueswell. 2005. Hard words. *Language Learning and Development*, 1(1):23–64.

Alison Gopnik and Andrew N. Meltzoff. 1997. Words, thoughts, and theories.

Alice A. Howard, Lara Mayeux, and Letitia R. Naigles. 2008. Conversational correlates of children's acquisition of mental verbs and a theory of mind. *First Language*, 28(4):375.

Carl Nils Johnson and Henry M. Wellman. 1980. Children's developing understanding of mental verbs: Remember, know, and guess. *Child Development*, 51(4):1095–1102.

Evan Kidd, Elena Lieven, and Michael Tomasello. 2006. Examining the role of lexical frequency in the acquisition and processing of sentential complements. *Cognitive Development*, 21(2):93–107.

Karin Kipper, Anna Korhonen, Neville Ryant, and Martha Palmer. 2008. A large-scale classification of English verbs. *Language Resources and Evaluation*, 42(1):21–40–40.

A. Kuczaj, Stan. 1977. The acquisition of regular and irregular past tense forms. *Journal of Verbal Learning and Verbal Behavior*, 16(5):589–600.

Elena Lieven, Dorothé Salomo, and Michael Tomasello. 2009. Two-year-old children's production of multiword utterances: A usage-based analysis. *Cognitive Linguistics*, 20(3):481–507.

Brian MacWhinney. 2000. *The CHILDES project: Tools for analyzing talk*, volume 2. Psychology Press.

Deborah G. Kemler Nelson, Kathy Hirsh-Pasek, Peter W. Jusczyk, and Kimberly Wright Cassidy. 1989. How the prosodic cues in motherese might assist language learning. *Journal of child Language*, 16(1):55–68.

Sourabh Niyogi. 2002. Bayesian learning at the syntax-semantics interface. In *Proceedings of the 24th Annual Conference of the Cognitive Science Society*.

Anna Papafragou, Kimberly Cassidy, and Lila Gleitman. 2007. When we think about thinking: The acquisition of belief verbs. *Cognition*, 105(1):125–165.

Christopher Parisien and Suzanne Stevenson. 2011. Generalizing between form and meaning using learned verb classes. In *Proceedings of the 33rd Annual Meeting of the Cognitive Science Society*.

Amy Perfors, Joshua B. Tenenbaum, and Elizabeth Wonnacott. 2010. Variability, negative evidence, and the acquisition of verb argument constructions. *Journal of Child Language*, 37(03):607–642.

Willard .V.O. Quine. 1960. *Word and object*, volume 4. The MIT Press.

Jacqueline Sachs. 1983. Talking about the there and then: The emergence of displaced reference in parent-child discourse. *Children's Language*, 4.

Marilyn Shatz, Henry M. Wellman, and Sharon Silber. 1983. The acquisition of mental verbs: A systematic investigation of the first reference to mental state. *Cognition*, 14(3):301–321.

Patrick Suppes. 1974. The semantics of children's language. *American Psychologist*, 29(2):103.

Semi-supervised learning for automatic conceptual property extraction

Colin Kelly
Computer Laboratory
University of Cambridge
Cambridge, CB3 0FD, UK
colin.kelly@cl.cam.ac.uk

Barry Devereux
Centre for Speech, Language, and the Brain
University of Cambridge
Cambridge, CB2 3EB, UK
barry@csl.psychol.cam.ac.uk

Anna Korhonen
Computer Laboratory
University of Cambridge
Cambridge, CB3 0FD, UK
anna.korhonen@cl.cam.ac.uk

Abstract

For a given concrete noun concept, humans are usually able to cite properties (e.g., *elephant is animal*, *car has wheels*) of that concept; cognitive psychologists have theorised that such properties are fundamental to understanding the abstract mental representation of concepts in the brain. Consequently, the ability to automatically extract such properties would be of enormous benefit to the field of experimental psychology. This paper investigates the use of semi-supervised learning and support vector machines to automatically extract concept-relation-feature triples from two large corpora (Wikipedia and UKWAC) for concrete noun concepts. Previous approaches have relied on manually-generated rules and hand-crafted resources such as WordNet; our method requires neither yet achieves better performance than these prior approaches, measured both by comparison with a property norm-derived gold standard as well as direct human evaluation. Our technique performs particularly well on extracting features relevant to a given concept, and suggests a number of promising areas for future focus.

1 Introduction

The representation of concrete concepts (e.g., **car**, **banana**, **spanner**) in the human brain has long been an important area of investigation for cognitive psychologists. Recent theories of this mental representation have proposed a componential, property-based and distributed model of conceptual knowledge (e.g., Farah and McClelland (1991), Randall et al. (2004), Tyler et al. (2000)).

In order to empirically test these cognitive theories, researchers have moved towards employing real-world knowledge in their experiments. This knowledge has usually been procured from human-derived lists of properties taken from property norming studies (Garrard et al., 2001; McRae et al., 2005). In such studies, human participants are asked to describe and note properties of a given concept (e.g., ***has** shell* for **turtle**). Synonymous responses are grouped together as a single property and those meeting a certain minimum response-frequency threshold are taken as valid properties. The most wide-ranging study to date was that conducted by McRae et al. (2005): some sample properties from this set are in Table 1.

As others have noted (Murphy, 2002; McRae et al., 2005), property norming studies are prone to a number of deficiencies. One such weakness is the incongruity of shared properties across even highly-related concepts: human respondents exhibit a lack of consistency when listing properties that are common to many similar concepts. For example, while ***has** legs* is listed as a property of **crocodile** in the McRae norms, it is absent as a property of **alligator**. A related issue is the non-comprehensive nature of the generated norms – although they may cover the most salient properties for a given concept, they are unlikely to comprise all of a concept's properties (e.g., ***has** heart* does not appear as a property of any of the 92 animal concepts).

Our research aims to use NLP techniques to create a system able to emulate the output of such studies, and overcome some of the aforementioned weaknesses. Our proposed system begins by searching dependency-parsed corpora for those sentences containing concept and feature terms which are also found in a McRae norm-derived training set of properties. For these sentences, the system generates grammatical relation/part-of-speech structural attributes and applies support vector machines (SVMs) to learn sets of attributes likely to indicate the instantiation of a property in a sentence. These

turtle		**bowl**	
has a shell	25	is round	19
lays eggs	16	used for eating	12
swims	15	used for soup	11
is green	14	used for food	11
lives in water	14	used for liquids	10
is slow	13	used for eating cereal	10
an animal	11	made of plastic	8
walks	10	used for holding things	7
walks slowly	10	is curved	7
has 4 legs	9	found in kitchens	7

Table 1: Top ten properties from McRae norms with production frequencies for **turtle** and **bowl**.

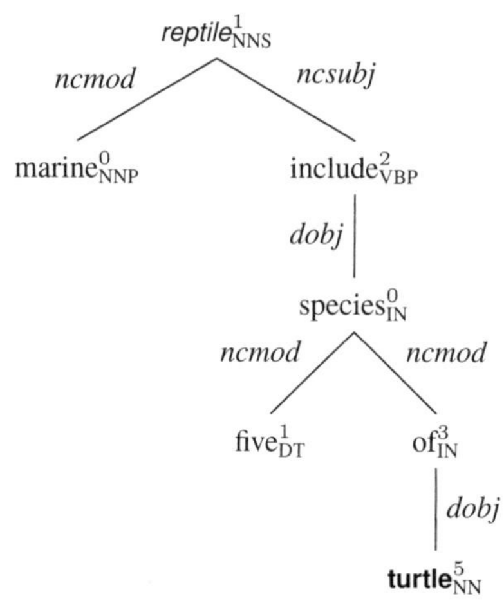

Figure 1: C&C-derived GR-POS graph for the sentence *Marine reptiles include five species of turtle.*

learned patterns of salient attributes are finally applied to a corpus to derive new properties for unseen concepts.

Our task is a challenging one: the properties we seek are extremely diverse in their form. They range from the simple (e.g., *banana is yellow*) to the complex (e.g., *bayonet found at the end of a gun*). Although the properties can broadly be divided into a number of categories (encyclopedic, taxonomic, functional, etc) there is not a great deal of regularity in the nature of the properties a given noun will likely possess: it is highly concept-dependent.

Furthermore, we hope to derive these properties from corpora, with the assumption that these properties will manifest themselves therein. Indeed, Andrews et al. (2005) discuss a theory of human knowledge which relies on a combination of both distributional (i.e., derived from spoken and written language) and experiential data (i.e., that derived from our interactions with the real world), claiming that the necessary contribution of each data-type for a comprehensive human semantic representation is non-trivial. Finally, there are difficulties associated with evaluating our system's output directly against a set of human-generated property norms: we discuss these in further detail later.

Given their provenance, the properties found in property norms are free-form. To simplify our task we apply a more rigid representation to the properties we already have and to those we aim to seek. We delineate each property into a **concept** ***relation*** *feature* triple (see Section 2.2) and our task becomes one of finding valid ***relation*** *feature* pairs given a particular **concept**. This recoding renders our task more well-defined and makes evaluation of our method more comparable to previous and related work.

Having framed our task in this way, there is an obvious parallel with relation extraction: both necessitate the selection/classification of relationships between individual entities (in our case, between **concept** and *feature*). Hearst (1992) was the first to propose a pattern-based approach to this task using lexico-syntactic patterns to automatically extract hyponyms and this technique has frequently been used for ontology learning. For example, Pantel and Pennacchiotti (2008) linked instantiations of a set of semantic relations into existing semantic ontologies and Davidov et al. (2007) employed seed concepts from a given semantic class to discover relations shared by concepts in that class.

Our task is more complex than classic relation extraction for two main reasons: 1) the relations which we aim to extract are not limited to a small set of just a few well-defined relations (e.g., ***is-a*** and ***part-of***) nor to the relations of a specific semantic class (e.g., ***capital-is*** for countries). Indeed the relations can be as many and diverse as the concepts themselves (e.g., each concept could possess a unique and distinguishing relation and feature). 2) We are attempting to simultaneously extract two pieces of information: features of the concept and those features' defining relationship with the concept, but only those relations and features which would be classified as 'common-sense', something which is easy for humans to recognise but difficult (if not impossible) to describe rigorously or formally.

There has recently been work on the automatic extraction of binary relations that scale to a web corpus, for example the ReVerb (Etzioni et al., 2011) and WOE (Wu and Weld, 2010) systems. These systems are designed to extract legitimate relations from a given sentence. In contrast, our aim is to capture more general relationships which are 'common-sense'; just because an extracted relation is correct in a given context does not automatically make it true in general. Previous reasoned approaches to our task have taken their lead from Hearst and her successors, employing manually-created rulesets to extract such properties from corpora (e.g., Baroni et al. (2009), Devereux et al. (2010), and our comparison system (Kelly et al., 2010)). Baroni et al. extract relational information in the form of 'type-sketches', which give an approximate, implicit description of the relationship whereas we are aiming to extract explicit relations between the target concept and its corresponding features. Devereux et al. and Kelly et al. have attempted this, but both employ WordNet (Fellbaum, 1998) to extract semantic relatedness information.

We use semi-supervised learning as it offers a flexible technique of harnessing small amounts of labelled data to derive information from unlabelled datasets/corpora and allows us to guide the extraction towards our desired 'common-sense' output. We chose SVMs as they have been used for a variety of tasks in NLP (e.g., Joachims et al. (1998), Giménez and Marquez (2004)). We will demonstrate that our system's performance exceeds that of Kelly et al. (2010) and Etzioni et al. (2011). It is, as far as we are aware, the first work to employ semi-supervised learning for this task.

2 Method

We will use SVMs to learn lexico-syntactic patterns in our corpora corresponding to known properties in order to find new ones. Training an SVM requires a labelled training set. To generate this set we harness our already-known concepts/features (and their relationships) from the McRae norms to find instantiations of said relationships within our corpora. We use parsed sentence information from our corpora to create a set of attributes describing each relationship, our learning patterns. In doing so, we are assuming that across sentences in our corpora containing a concept/feature pair found in the McRae norms, there will be a set of consistent lexico-syntactic patterns which indicate the same relationship as that linking the pair in the norms.

Thus we iterate over our chosen corpora, parsing each concept-containing sentence to yield grammatical relation (GR) and part-of-speech (POS) information from which we can create a GR-POS graph relating the two. Then for each triple, we find any/all paths through the graph which link the **concept** to its *feature* and use the corresponding ***relation*** to label this path. We collect descriptive information about the path in the form of attributes describing it (e.g., path nodes, labels, length) to create a training pattern specific to that **concept** ***relation*** *feature* triple and sentence. It is these lists of attributes (and their ***relation*** labels) which we employ as the labelled training set and as input for our SVM.

2.1 Corpora

We employ two corpora for our experiments: Wikipedia and the UKWAC corpus (Ferraresi et al., 2008). These are both publicly available and web-based: the former a source of encyclopedic information and the latter a source of general text. Our Wikipedia corpus is based on a Sep 2009 version of English-language Wikipedia and contains around 1.84 million articles (>1bn words). Our UKWAC corpus is an English-language corpus (>2bn words) obtained by crawling the `.uk` internet domain.

2.2 Training data

Our experiments use a British-English version of the McRae norms (see Taylor et al. (2011) for details). We needed to recode the free-form McRae properties into relation-classes and features which would be usable for our learning algorithm. As we will be matching the features from these properties with individual words in the training corpus it was essential that the features we generated contained only one lemmatised word. In contrast, the relations were merely labels for the relationship described (they did not need to occur in the sentences we were training from) and therefore needed only to be single-string relations. This allowed prepositional verbs as distinct relations, something which has not been attempted in previous work yet can be semantically significant (e.g., the relations ***used-in***, ***used-for*** and ***used-by*** have dissimilar meanings).

We applied the following sequential multi-step

process to our set of free-form properties to distill them to triples of the form **concept *relation*** *feature*, where ***relation*** can be a multi-word string and *feature* is a single word:

1. Translation of implicit properties to their correct relations (e.g., *pig an animal* → *pig is an animal*).
2. Removal of indefinite and definite articles.
3. Behavioural properties become "does" properties (e.g., *turtle beh eats* → *turtle does eats*).
4. Negative properties given their own relation classes (e.g., *turkey does cannot fly* → *turkey doesnt fly*).
5. All numbers are translated to named cardinals (e.g., *spider has 8 legs* → *spider has eight legs*).
6. Some of the norms already contained synonymous terms: these were split into separate triples for each synonym (e.g., *pepper tastes hot/spicy* → *pepper tastes hot* and *pepper tastes spicy*).
7. Prepositional verbs were translated to one-word, hyphenated strings (e.g., *made of* → *made-of*).
8. Properties with present participles as the penultimate word were split into one including the verb as the feature and one including it in the relation (e.g., *envelope used for sending letters* → *envelope used-for-sending letters* and *envelope used-for sending*).
9. Any remaining multi-word properties were split with the first term after the concept acting as the relation (e.g., *bull has ring in its nose* → *bull has ring*, *bull has in*, *bull has its* and *bull has nose*).
10. All remaining stop-words were removed; properties ending in stop-words (e.g., *bull has in* and *bull has its*) were removed completely.

This yielded 7,518 property-triples with 254 distinct relations and an average of 14.7 triples per concept.

2.3 Parsing

We parsed both corpora using the C&C parser (Clark and Curran, 2007) as we employ both GR and POS information in our learning method. To accelerate this stage, we process only sentences containing a form (e.g., singular/plural) of one of our training/testing concepts. We lemmatise each word using the WordNet NLTK lemmatiser (Bird, 2006). Parsing our corpora yields around 10Gb and 12Gb of data for UKWAC and Wikipedia respectively.

The C&C dependency parse output contains, for a given sentence, a set of GRs forming an acyclic graph whose nodes correspond to words from the sentence, with each node also labelled with the POS of that word. Thus the GR-POS graph interrelates all lexical, POS and GR information for the entire sentence. It is therefore possible to construct a GR-POS graph rooted at our target term (the concept in question), with POS-labelled words as nodes, and edges labelled with GRs linking the nodes to one another. An example graph can be seen in Figure 1.

2.4 Support vector machines

We use SVMs (Cortes and Vapnik, 1995) for our experiments as they have been widely used in NLP and their properties are well-understood, showing good performance on classification tasks (Meyer et al., 2003). In their canonical form, SVMs are non-probabilistic binary linear classifiers which take a set of input data and predict, for each given input, which of two possible classes it corresponds to.

There are more than two possible relation-labels to learn for our input patterns, so ours is a multi-class classification task. For our experiments we use the SVM Light Multiclass (v. 2.20) software (Joachims, 1999) which applies the fixed-point SVM algorithm described by Crammer and Singer (2002) to solve multi-class problem instances. Joachims' software has been widely used to implement SVMs (Vinokourov et al., 2003; Godbole et al., 2002).

2.5 Attribute selection

Previous techniques for our task have made use of lexical, syntactic and semantic information. We are deliberately avoiding the use of manually-created semantic resources, so we rely only on lexical and syntactic attributes for our learning stage (i.e., the GR-POS paths described earlier).

A table of all the categories of attributes we extract for each GR-POS path are in Table 2.4, together with attributes from the path linking **turtle** and *reptile* in our example sentence (see Figure 1).

We ran our experiments with two vector-types which we call our 'verb-augmented' and our 'non-augmented' vector-types. The sets are identical except the verb-augmented vector-type will also contain an additional attribute category containing an attribute for every instance of a relation verb (i.e., a verb which is found in our training set of relations, e.g., *become*, *cause*, *taste*, *use*, *have* and so on) in the lexical path. We do this to ascertain whether this additional verb-information might be more informative to our system when learning relations (which tend to be composed of verbs).

Attribute category	Example attribute(s)
GR path-length	LEN
lemmatised anchor node	LEM=turtle
POS of anchor node	POS=NN
GR path labels from anchor (indexed)	GR1=dobjR GR2=ncmodR GR3=dobjR GR4=ncsubjN
GR path labels from target (indexed)	GR1=ncsubjR GR2=dobjN GR3=ncmodN GR4=dobjN
POS of path nodes from anchor (indexed)	POS1=IN POS2=NNS POS3=VBP POS4=NNS
POS of path nodes from target (indexed)	POS1=NNS POS2=VBP POS3=NNS POS4=IN
lemmatised path nodes (bag of words)	LEM=include LEM=species LEM=of
POS of all path nodes (set)	POS=IN POS=NNS POS=VBP
Relation verbs	N/A
GR path labels (set)	GR=dobjR GR=ncmodN GR=ncsubjN
lemmatised target node	LEM=reptile
POS of target node	POS=NNS

Table 2: An example vector for an instance of the relation-label ***is***. The attributes are distinguished from one another by their attribute category. Relation verbs only appear in the verb-augmented vector-type and no such verbs appear in our example sentence, so this category of attribute is empty. All attributes in the table will receive the value `1.0` except the `LEN` attribute which will have the value `0.2` (the reciprocal of the path length, 5).

We considered allocating a 'no-rel' relation label to those sets of attributes corresponding to paths through the GR-POS graph which did *not* link the concept to a feature found in our training data; however our initial experiments indicated the SVM model would assign every pattern we tested to the 'no-rel' relation. Therefore we used only positive instances in our training pattern data.

We cycle through all training concepts/features, finding sentences containing both. For each such sentence, our system generates the attributes from the GR-POS path linking the concept to the feature (the linking-path) to create a pattern for that pair, in the form of a relation-labelled vector containing real-valued attributes. The system assigns `1.0` to all attributes occurring in a given path and the `LEN` value receives the reciprocal of the path-length.[1] Each linking-path is collected into a ***relation***-labelled, sparse vector in this manner. In the larger UKWAC corpus this corresponds to over 29 million unique attributes across all found linking-paths (this figure corresponds to the dimensionality of our vectors). We then pass all vectors to the learning module[2] of SVM Light to generate a learned model across all training concepts.

2.6 Extracting candidate patterns

Having trained our model, we must now find potential features and relations for our test concepts in our corpora. We again only examine sentences which contain at least one of our test concepts. Furthermore, to avoid a combinatorial explosion of possible paths rooted at those concepts we only permit as candidates those paths whose anchor node is a singular or plural noun and whose target node is either a singular/plural noun or adjective. This filtering corresponds to choosing patterns containing one of the three most frequent anchor node POS tags (`NN`, `NNS` and `NNP`) and target node POS tags (`NN`, `JJ` and `NNS`) found during our training stage. These candidate patterns constitute 92.6% and 87.7% of all the vectors, respectively, from our training set of patterns (on the UKWAC corpus). This pattern pre-selection allows us to immediately ignore paths which, despite being rooted at a test concept, are unlikely to contain property norm-like information.

2.7 Generating and ranking triples

We next classified our test concepts' candidate patterns using the learned model. SVM Light assigns each pattern a relation-class from the training set and outputs the values of the decision functions from the learned model when applied to that particular pattern. The sign of these values indicates the binary decision function choice, and their magnitude acts as a measure of confidence. We wanted those vectors which the model was most confident in across all decision functions, so we took the sum of the absolute values of the decision values to generate a pattern score for each vector/relation-label.

[1] All other possible attributes are assigned the value `0.0`.

[2] Using a regularisation parameter (`C`) value of 1.0 and default parameters otherwise.

	Vector-type	Corpus	β_{LL}	β_{PMI}	β_{SVM}	Prec.	Recall	F
Ignoring relation.	Non-augmented	Wikipedia	0.3	0.00	1.00	0.2214	0.3197	0.2564
		UKWAC	0.10	0.05	0.60	0.2279	0.3330	0.2664
		UKWAC-Wikipedia	0.35	0.00	0.75	0.2422	0.3533	0.2829
	Verb-augmented	Wikipedia	0.20	0.00	0.65	0.2217	0.3202	0.2568
		UKWAC	0.30	0.00	0.95	0.2326	0.3400	0.2720
		UKWAC-Wikipedia	**0.40**	**0.05**	**1.00**	**0.2444**	**0.3577**	**0.2859**
With relation.	Non-augmented	Wikipedia	0.05	0.00	1.00	0.1199	0.1732	0.1394
		UKWAC	0.05	0.00	1.00	0.1126	0.1633	0.1312
		UKWAC-Wikipedia	0.05	0.00	0.65	0.1241	0.1808	0.1449
	Verb-augmented	Wikipedia	0.05	0.00	1.00	0.1215	0.1747	0.1410
		UKWAC	0.05	0.00	1.00	0.1190	0.1724	0.1387
		UKWAC-Wikipedia	**0.05**	**0.00**	**0.70**	**0.1281**	**0.1860**	**0.1494**

Table 3: Parameter estimation both with and without relation, using our augmented and non-augmented vector-types and across our two corpora and the combined corpora set.

From these patterns we derived an output set of triples where the concept and feature of a triple corresponded to the anchor and target nodes of its pattern and the relation corresponded to the pattern's relation-label. Identical triples from differing patterns had their pattern scores summed to give a final 'SVM score' for that triple.

2.8 Calculating triple scores

A brief qualitative evaluation of our system's output indicates that although the higher-ranked (by SVM score) features and relations were, for the most part, quite sensible, there were some obvious output errors (e.g., non-dictionary strings or verbs appearing as features). Therefore we restricted our features to those which appear as nouns or adjectives in WordNet and excluded features containing an NLTK (Bird, 2006) corpus stop-word. Despite these exclusions, some general (and therefore less informative) relation/feature combinations (e.g., ***is*** *good*, ***is*** *new*) were still ranking highly. To mitigate this, we extract both log-likelihood (LL) and pointwise mutual information (PMI) scores for each concept/feature pair to assess the relative saliency of each extracted feature, with a view to downweighting common but less interesting features. To speed up this and later stages, we calculate both statistics for the top 1,000 triples extracted for each concept only.

PMI was proposed by Church and Hanks (1990) to estimate word association. We will use it to measure the strength of association between a concept and its feature. We hope that emphasising concept-feature pairs with high mutual information will render our triples more relevant/informative.

We also employ the LL measure across our set of concept-feature pairs. Proposed by Dunning (1993), LL is a measure of the distribution of linguistic phenomena in texts and has been used to contrast the relative corpus frequencies of words. Our aim is to highlight features which are particularly distinctive for a given concept, and hence likely to be features of that concept alone.

We calculate an overall score for a triple, t, by a weighted combination of the triple's SVM, PMI and LL scores using the following formula:

$$\mathrm{score}(t) = \beta_{\mathrm{PMI}} \cdot \mathrm{PMI}(t) + \beta_{\mathrm{LL}} \cdot \mathrm{LL}(t) + \beta_{\mathrm{SVM}} \cdot \mathrm{SVM}(t)$$

where the PMI, SVM and LL scores are normalised so they are in the range [0, 1]. The relative β weights thus give an estimate of the three measures' importance relative to one another and allows us to gauge which combination of these scores is optimal.

2.9 Datasets

We also wanted to ascertain the extent to which the output from both our corpora could be combined to improve results, balancing the encyclopedic but somewhat specific nature of Wikipedia with the generality and breadth of the UKWAC corpus. We combined the output by summing individual SVM scores of each triple from both corpora to yield a combined SVM score. PMI and LL scores were then calculated as usual from this combined set of triples.

3 Experimental Evaluation

3.1 Evaluation methodology

We employ ten-fold cross-validation to ascertain optimal SVM, LL and PMI β parameters for our final system. We exclude 44 concepts from our set of

	Relation	Prec.	Recall	F
Kelly et al.	Without	0.1943	0.3896	0.2592
	With	0.1102	0.2210	0.1471
ReVerb	Without	0.1142	0.2258	0.1514
	With	0.0431	0.0864	0.0576
Our method	Without	0.2417	0.4847	0.3225
	With	0.1238	0.2493	0.1654

Table 4: Our best scores on the ESSLLI set compared to Kelly et al. (2010) and the ReVerb system (Etzioni et al., 2011). Our results are from the verb-augmented vector-type, using the combined UKWAC-Wikipedia corpus and using the β parameters highlighted in Table 3.

510 to use in our final system testing and split the remaining 466 concepts randomly and evenly into 10 folds. We apply the training steps above to nine of the folds, generating predictions for the single held-out fold. We repeat this for all ten folds, yielding relations and features with SVM, LL and PMI scores for our full set of 466 training concepts on the UKWAC, Wikipedia and combined corpora.

We varied the β values from our scoring equation in the range [0,1] (interval 0.05) and compared the top twenty triples for each concept directly against the held-out training set. The best F-scores and their corresponding β values (evaluating on full triples and concept-feature pairs alone) are in Table 3. We can see that our best results employ the verb-augmented vector-type and the combined corpus, with a best F-score of 0.2859 when ignoring the relation term and 0.1494 when including it in the evaluation. The main difference between these two results is the relative contribution of the reweighting factors: the SVM score is the most important overall, but the LL and PMI scores come into play when evaluating without the relation. This could be explained by the fact that the PMI and LL scores do not use any relation terms in their calculations.

3.2 Quantitative evaluation

The unseen subset of the McRae norms is a set of human-generated common-sense properties with which our extracted properties can be compared. However, an issue with the McRae norms is that semantically identical properties can be represented by lexically different triples. This problem was acknowledged by Baroni et al. (2008) who created a synonym-expanded set of properties for 44 concepts (selected evenly across six semantic classes; the 44 concepts we excluded for testing) to partially solve it. This expansion set comprises the concepts' top ten properties from the McRae norms with semi-automatically generated synonyms for each of the ten distinct features. For example, the triple **turtle *has*** *shell* was expanded to also include **turtle *has*** *shield* and **turtle *has*** *carapace*.

	Judge			Judge	
turtle	A	B	**bowl**	A	B
is *green*	c	c	***is*** *large*	p	p
is *small*	c	c	***used for*** *food*	c	c
is *species*	c	c	***used for*** *mixing*	c	c
is *marine*	c	c	***used for storing*** *food*	c	c
used for *sea*	r	r	***used for storing*** *soup*	r	r
is *animal*	c	c	***is*** *ceramic*	c	c
is *many*	p	c	***is*** *small*	p	p
has *shell*	c	c	***used for storing*** *cereal*	r	r
is *large*	c	p	***used for storing*** *spoon*	r	r
is *reptile*	c	c	***used for storing*** *sugar*	p	c

Table 5: Our judges' assessments of the correctness of the top ten relation/feature pairs for two concepts extracted from our best system.

We use the two best systems (i.e., including and excluding the relation; highlighted in Table 3) to generate two sets of top twenty output triples for our 44 concepts. We then calculate precision, recall and F-scores for each against our synonym-expanded set.[3] Using this expanded set allows us to compare our work with that of Kelly et al. (2010). We also compare with the top twenty output of the Reverb system Etzioni et al. (2011) using their publicly available relations derived from the ClueWeb09 corpus, employing their normalized triples ranked by frequency. All sets of results are in Table 4. We note that even though Kelly et al. optimised their algorithm on the ESSLLI set to yield a theoretical best-possible score—we are evaluating 'blind'—our performance still shows an advance on theirs: the improvement on both sets when comparing the population of F-scores across all 44 concepts is statistically significant at the 0.5% level.[4]

3.3 Human evaluation

The above does not quite offer the full picture: unlike the features, the relations are not synonym-expanded. Furthermore, it is possible that there

[3]We note that we are incorporating an upper bound for precision of 0.500 by comparing with only the top ten properties.

[4]Paired t-tests. 'With relation': $t = 3.524$, d.f.$= 43$, $p = 0.0010$. 'Without relation': $t = 3.503$, d.f.$= 43$, $p = 0.0011$.

Relation		A	B	κ	Agreements
With	c / p	146	161	0.7421	261 (87%)
	r / w	153	138		
Without	c / p	226	235	0.5792	255 (85%)
	r / w	74	65		

Table 6: Inter-annotator agreement for our best system, both including and excluding the relation.

are correct properties being generated which simply don't appear in the ESSLLI evaluation set.

In order to address these concerns, we also performed a human evaluation on 15 of our concepts.[5] We asked two native English-speaking judges to decide whether a given triple was *correct*,[6] *plausible*,[7] *wrong but related*,[8] or *wrong*.[9] We executed the human evaluation on our two best systems (as described above). As there were shared triples and concept-feature pairs across the two output sets, each triple and pair was evaluated only once. The judges were aware of the purposes of the study but were blind to the source sets. Some example judgements are in Table 5.

The agreement results across all 15 concepts together with their κ coefficients (Cohen, 1960) are in Table 6. In our evaluation we conflated the *correct/plausible* and *wrong but related/wrong* categories (see also Kelly et al. (2010) and Devereux et al. (2010)). We did this because of the subjective nature of the judgements, and because we are seeking properties which are indeed correct or at least plausible. These results indicate that our system is extracting correct or plausible triples 51.1% of the time (rising to 76.8% when considering features only). They also demonstrate a marked discrepancy between the results for our two evaluations, reflecting the necessity of human evaluation when assessing our particular task.

4 Discussion

In this paper we have shown that semi-supervised learning techniques can automatically learn lexico-syntactic patterns indicative of property norm-like relations and features. Using these patterns, our system can extract relevant and accurate properties from any parsed corpus and allows for multi-word relation labels, allowing greater semantic precision.

As already mentioned, the work of Baroni et al. (2009) is relevant to our own. Their approach achieves a precision score of 0.239 on the top ten returned features evaluated against the ESSLLI set: our best system offers precision of 0.370 on the same evaluation. Moreover, Baroni et al. do not explicitly derive relation terms. We better the performance of a comparable system (Kelly et al., 2010), even when evaluating against an unseen set of concepts, and our system does not use manually-generated rules or semantic information. Furthermore, human evaluation shows over half of our extracted properties are correct/plausible.

For future work, we have already mentioned that we are ignoring a large amount of potentially instructive training data, specifically those GR-POS paths in our corpus which don't terminate on one of our training features, as well as those paths through sentences containing one of our concepts but none of our training features. It might therefore be worthwhile investigating the use of this "negative" information. Another potential avenue for exploration would be the expansion of the learning vector-types. Although we already use a significant number of learning attributes (an average of 37.9 per training pattern), we could include more: there may be additional information not directly on the GR-POS path linking a concept and feature (e.g., nodes adjacent to said path) which might be indicative of their relationship. We would also consider using active-learning, introducing a feedback loop and human-annotation to better distinguish between relations which our algorithm tends to classify incorrectly. For example, we could supplement input pattern data with disambiguating POS-GR graphs, drawing a distinction between valid and non-valid relations.

Finally, our system could also be evaluated in the context of a psycholinguistic experiment. For example, we could use our system output to predict concept similarity by using our extracted triples to create vector representations of each concept, calculating the distance between those vectors and comparing these similarity ratings with human judgements.

[5]The 44 evaluation concepts had been separated into superordinate categories for unrelated psycholinguistic research and we selected our 15 proportionally and at random from these superordinate categories.

[6]A correct, valid, feature.

[7]A triple which is plausible but only in a specific set of circumstances or a feature which was correct but very general.

[8]The triple is incorrect but there existed some sort of relationship between the concept and relation and/or feature.

[9]When the triple is simply wrong.

Acknowledgements

This research was supported by EPSRC grant EP/F030061/1. We are grateful to McRae and colleagues for making their norms publicly available, and to the anonymous reviewers for their helpful input.

References

M. Andrews, G. Vigliocco, and D. Vinson. 2005. Integrating attributional and distributional information in a probabilistic model of meaning representation. In Timo Honkela et al., editor, *Proceedings of AKRR'05, International and Interdisciplinary Conference on Adaptive Knowledge Representation and Reasoning*, pages 15–25, Espoo, Finland: Helsinki University of Technology.

M. Baroni, S. Evert, and A. Lenci, editors. 2008. *ESSLLI 2008 Workshop on Distributional Lexical Semantics*.

M. Baroni, B. Murphy, Barbu E., and Poesio M. 2009. Strudel: A corpus-based semantic model based on properties and types. *Cognitive Science*, pages 1–33.

S. Bird. 2006. NLTK: The natural language toolkit. In *Proceedings of the COLING/ACL on Interactive presentation sessions*, pages 69–72. Association for Computational Linguistics.

K.W. Church and P. Hanks. 1990. Word association norms, mutual information, and lexicography. *Computational Linguistics*, 16(1):22–29.

S. Clark and J.R. Curran. 2007. Wide-coverage efficient statistical parsing with CCG and log-linear models. *Computational Linguistics*, 33(4):493–552.

J. Cohen. 1960. A coefficient of agreement for nominal scales. *Educational and psychological measurement*.

C. Cortes and V. Vapnik. 1995. Support-vector networks. *Machine learning*, 20(3):273–297.

K. Crammer and Y. Singer. 2002. On the algorithmic implementation of multiclass kernel-based vector machines. *The Journal of Machine Learning Research*, 2:265–292.

D. Davidov, A. Rappoport, and M. Koppel. 2007. Fully unsupervised discovery of concept-specific relationships by web mining. In *Annual Meeting-Association For Computational Linguistics*, volume 45, page 232.

B. Devereux, N. Pilkington, T. Poibeau, and A. Korhonen. 2010. Towards unrestricted, large-scale acquisition of feature-based conceptual representations from corpus data. *Research on Language & Computation*, pages 1–34.

T. Dunning. 1993. Accurate methods for the statistics of surprise and coincidence. *Computational linguistics*, 19(1):61–74.

O. Etzioni, A. Fader, J. Christensen, S. Soderland, and M.T. Center. 2011. Open information extraction: The second generation. In *Twenty-Second International Joint Conference on Artificial Intelligence*.

M.J. Farah and J.L. McClelland. 1991. A computational model of semantic memory impairment: Modality specificity and emergent category specificity. *Journal of Experimental Psychology: General*, 120(4):339–357.

C. Fellbaum. 1998. *WordNet: An electronic lexical database*. The MIT press.

A. Ferraresi, E. Zanchetta, M. Baroni, and S. Bernardini. 2008. Introducing and evaluating ukwac, a very large web-derived corpus of english. In *Proceedings of the 4th Web as Corpus Workshop (WAC-4) Can we beat Google*, pages 47–54.

P. Garrard, M.A.L. Ralph, J.R. Hodges, and K. Patterson. 2001. Prototypicality, distinctiveness, and intercorrelation: Analyses of the semantic attributes of living and nonliving concepts. *Cognitive Neuropsychology*, 18(2):125–174.

J. Giménez and L. Marquez. 2004. Svmtool: A general pos tagger generator based on support vector machines. In *In Proceedings of the 4th International Conference on Language Resources and Evaluation*. Citeseer.

S. Godbole, S. Sarawagi, and S. Chakrabarti. 2002. Scaling multi-class support vector machines using inter-class confusion. In *Proceedings of the eighth ACM SIGKDD international conference on Knowledge discovery and data mining*, pages 513–518. ACM.

M.A. Hearst. 1992. Automatic acquisition of hyponyms from large text corpora. In *Proceedings of the 14th conference on Computational linguistics-Volume 2*, pages 539–545. Association for Computational Linguistics.

T. Joachims, C. Nedellec, and C. Rouveirol. 1998. Text categorization with support vector machines: learning with many relevant. In *Machine Learning: ECML-98 10th European Conference on Machine Learning, Chemnitz, Germany*, pages 137–142. Springer.

T. Joachims. 1999. Svmlight: Support vector machine. *SVM-Light Support Vector Machine http://svmlight.joachims.org/, University of Dortmund*, 19.

C. Kelly, B. Devereux, and A. Korhonen. 2010. Acquiring human-like feature-based conceptual representations from corpora. In *First Workshop on Computational Neurolinguistics*, page 61. Citeseer.

K. McRae, G.S. Cree, M.S. Seidenberg, and C. McNorgan. 2005. Semantic feature production norms for a large set of living and nonliving things. *Behavioral Research Methods, Instruments, and Computers*, 37:547–559.

D. Meyer, F. Leisch, and K. Hornik. 2003. The support vector machine under test. *Neurocomputing*, 55(1-2):169–186.

G. Murphy. 2002. *The big book of concepts*. The MIT Press, Cambridge, MA.

P. Pantel and M. Pennacchiotti. 2008. Automatically harvesting and ontologizing semantic relations. In *Proceeding of the 2008 conference on Ontology Learning and Population: Bridging the Gap between Text and Knowledge*, pages 171–195. IOS Press.

B. Randall, H.E. Moss, J.M. Rodd, M. Greer, and L.K. Tyler. 2004. Distinctiveness and correlation in conceptual structure: Behavioral and computational studies. *Journal of Experimental Psychology Learning Memory and Cognition*, 30(2):393–406.

K.I. Taylor, B.J. Devereux, K. Acres, B. Randall, and L.K. Tyler. 2011. Contrasting effects of feature-based statistics on the categorisation and basic-level identification of visual objects. *Cognition*.

L.K. Tyler, H.E. Moss, M.R. Durrant-Peatfield, and J.P. Levy. 2000. Conceptual structure and the structure of concepts: A distributed account of category-specific deficits. *Brain and Language*, 75(2):195–231.

A. Vinokourov, J. Shawe-Taylor, and N. Cristianini. 2003. Inferring a semantic representation of text via cross-language correlation analysis. *Advances in neural information processing systems*, 15:1473–1480.

F. Wu and D.S. Weld. 2010. Open information extraction using wikipedia. In *Proceedings of the 48th Annual Meeting of the Association for Computational Linguistics*, pages 118–127. Association for Computational Linguistics.

Why long words take longer to read: the role of uncertainty about word length

Klinton Bicknell
Department of Psychology
University of California, San Diego
9500 Gilman Drive #109
La Jolla, CA 92093-0109
kbicknell@ucsd.edu

Roger Levy
Department of Linguistics
University of California, San Diego
9500 Gilman Drive #108
La Jolla, CA 92093-0108
rlevy@ucsd.edu

Abstract

Some of the most robust effects of linguistic variables on eye movements in reading are those of word length. Their leading explanation states that they are caused by visual acuity limitations on word recognition. However, Bicknell (2011) presented data showing that a model of eye movement control in reading that includes visual acuity limitations and models the process of word identification from visual input (Bicknell & Levy, 2010) does not produce humanlike word length effects, providing evidence against the visual acuity account. Here, we argue that uncertainty about word length in early word identification can drive word length effects. We present an extension of Bicknell and Levy's model that incorporates word length uncertainty, and show that it produces more humanlike word length effects.

1 Introduction

Controlling the eyes while reading is a complex task, and doing so efficiently requires rapid decisions about when and where to move the eyes 3–4 times per second. Research in psycholinguistics has demonstrated that these decisions are sensitive to a range of linguistic properties of the text being read, suggesting that the eye movement record may be viewed as a detailed trace of the timecourse of incremental comprehension. A number of cognitive models of eye movement control in reading have been proposed, the most well-known of which are E-Z Reader (Reichle, Pollatsek, Fisher, & Rayner, 1998; Reichle, Rayner, & Pollatsek, 2003) and SWIFT (Engbert, Longtin, & Kliegl, 2002; Engbert, Nuthmann, Richter, & Kliegl, 2005). These models capture a large range of the known properties of eye movements in reading, including effects of the best-documented linguistic variables on eye movements: the frequency, predictability, and length of words.

Both models assume that word frequency, predictability, and length affect eye movements in reading by affecting word recognition, yet neither one models the process of identifying words from visual information. Rather, each of these models directly specifies the effects of these variables on exogenous word processing functions, and the eye movements the models produce are sensitive to these functions' output. Thus, this approach cannot answer the question of *why* these linguistic variables have the effects they do on eye movement behavior. Recently, Bicknell and Levy (2010) presented a model of eye movement control in reading that directly models the process of identifying the text from visual input, and makes eye movements to maximize the efficiency of the identification process. Bicknell and Levy (2012) demonstrated that this rational model produces effects of word frequency and predictability that qualitatively match those of humans: words that are less frequent and less predictable receive more and longer fixations. Because this model makes eye movements to maximize the efficiency of the identification process, this result gives an answer for the reason why these variables should have the effects that they do on eye movement behavior: a model that works to efficiently identify the text makes more and longer fixations on words of lower frequency and predictability because it needs more visual information to identify them.

Bicknell (2011) showed, however, that the effects of word length produced by the rational model look quite different from those of human readers. Because Bicknell and Levy's (2010) model implements the main proposal for why word length effects should arise, i.e., visual acuity limitations, the fact that the model does not reproduce humanlike word length effects suggests that our understanding of the causes of word length effects may be incomplete.

In this paper, we argue that this result arose because of a simplifying assumption made in the rational model, namely, the assumption that the reader has veridical knowledge about the number of characters in a word being identified. We present an extension of Bicknell and Levy's (2010) model which does not make this simplifying assumption, and show in two sets of simulations that effects of word length produced by the extended model look more like those of humans. We argue from these results that uncertainty about word length is a necessary component of a full understanding of word length effects in reading.

2 Reasons for word length effects

The empirical effects of word length displayed by human readers are simple to describe: longer words receive more and longer fixations. The major reason proposed in the literature on eye movements in reading for this effect is that when fixating longer words, the average visual acuity of all the letters in the word will be lower than for shorter words, and this poorer average acuity is taken to lead to longer and more fixations. This intuition is built into the exogenous word processing functions in E-Z Reader and SWIFT. Specifically, in both models, the word processing rate slows as the average distance to the fovea of all letters in the word increases, and this specification of the effect of length on word processing rates is enough to produce reasonable effects of word length on eye movements: both models make more and longer fixations on longer words – similar to the pattern of humans – across a range of measures (Pollatsek, Reichle, & Rayner, 2006; Engbert et al., 2005) including the duration of the first fixation on a word (first fixation duration), the duration of all fixations on a word prior to leaving the word (gaze duration), the rate at which a word is not fixated prior to a fixation on a word beyond it (skip rate), and the rate with which a word is fixated more than once prior to a word beyond it (refixation rate).

There are, however, reasons to believe that this account may be incomplete. First, while it is the case that the average visual acuity of all letters in a fixated word must be lower for longer words, this is just because there are additional letters in the longer word. While these additional letters pull down the average visual acuity of letters within the word, each additional letter should still provide additional visual information about the word's identity, an argument suggesting that longer words might require less – not more – time to be identified. In fact, in SWIFT, the exogenous word processing rate function slows as both the average and the sum of the visual acuities of the letters within the word decrease, but E-Z Reader does not implement this idea in any way. Additionally, a factor absent from both E-Z Reader and SWIFT, is that the visual neighborhoods of longer words (at least in English) appear to be sparser, when considering the number of words formed by a single letter substitution (Balota, Cortese, Sergent-Marshall, Spieler, & Yap, 2004), or the average orthographic Levenshtein distance of the most similar 20 words (Yarkoni, Balota, & Yap, 2008). Because reading words with more visual neighbors is generally slower (Pollatsek, Perea, & Binder, 1999), this argument gives another reason to expect longer words to require less – not more – time to be read.

So while E-Z Reader and SWIFT produce reasonable effects of word length on eye movement measures (in which longer words receive more and longer fixations) by assuming a particular effect of visual acuity, it is less clear whether a visual acuity account can yield reasonable word length effects in a model that also includes the two opposing effects mentioned above. Determining how these different factors should interact to produce word length effects requires a model of eye movements in reading that models the process of word identification from disambiguating visual input (Bicknell & Levy, in press). The model presented by Bicknell and Levy (2010) fits this description, and includes visual acuity limitations (in fact, identical to the visual acuity function in SWIFT). As already mentioned, however, Bicknell (2011) showed that the model did not yield a humanlike length effect. Instead, while longer words were skipped less often and refixated more (as for humans), fixation durations generally fell with word length – the opposite of the pattern shown by humans. This result suggests that visual acuity limitations alone cannot explain the positive effect of word length on fixation durations in the presence of an opposing force such as the fact that longer words have smaller visual neighborhoods.

We hypothesize that the reason for this pattern of results relates to a simplifying assumption made by Bicknell and Levy's model. Specifically, while visual input in the model yields noisy information about the identities of letters, it gives veridical information about the number of letters in each word, for reasons of computational convenience. There are theoretical and empirical reasons to believe that this simplifying assumption is incorrect, that early in the word identification process human readers do have substantial uncertainty about the number of letters in a word, and further, that this may be especially so for long words. For example, results with masked priming have shown that recognition of a target word is facilitated by a prime that is a proper subset of the target's letters (e.g., blcn–balcon; Peressotti & Grainger, 1999; Grainger, Granier, Farioli, Van Assche, & van Heuven, 2006), providing evidence that words of different length have substantial similarity in early processing. For these reasons, some recent models of isolated word recognition (Gomez, Ratcliff, & Perea, 2008; Norris, Kinoshita, & van Casteren, 2010) have suggested that readers have some uncertainty about the number of letters in a word early in processing.

If readers have uncertainty about the length of words, we may expect that the amount of uncertainty would grow proportionally to length, as uncertainty is proportional to set size in other tasks of number estimation (Dehaene, 1997). This would agree with the intuition that an 8-character word should be more easily confused with a 9-character word than a 3-character word with a 4-character word. Including uncertainty about word length that is larger for longer words would have the effect of increasing the number of visual neighbors for longer words more than for shorter words, providing another reason (in addition to visual acuity limitations) that longer words may require more and longer fixations.

In the remainder of this paper, we describe an extension of Bicknell and Levy's (2010) model in which visual input provides stochastic – rather than veridical – information about the length of words, yielding uncertainty about word length, and in which the amount of uncertainty grows with length. We then present two sets of simulations with this extended model demonstrating that it produces more humanlike effects of word length, suggesting that uncertainty about word length may be an important component of a full understanding of the effects of word length in reading.

3 A rational model of reading

In this section, we describe our extension of Bicknell and Levy's (2010) rational model of eye movement control in reading. Except for the visual input system, and a small change to the behavior policy to allow for uncertainty about word length, the model is identical to that described by Bicknell and Levy. The reader is referred to that paper for further computational details beyond what is described here.

In this model, the goal of reading is taken to be efficient text identification. While it is clear that this is not all that readers do – inferring the underlying structural relationships among words in a sentence and discourse relationships between sentences that determine text meaning is a fundamental part of most reading – all reader goals necessarily involve identification of at least part of the text, so text identification is taken to be a reasonable first approximation. There are two sources of information relevant to this goal: visual input and language knowledge, which the model combines via Bayesian inference. Specifically, it begins with a prior distribution over possible identities of the text given by its language model, and combines this with noisy visual input about the text at the eyes' position, giving the likelihood term, to form a posterior distribution over the identity of the text taking into account both the language model and the visual input obtained thus far. On the basis of the posterior distribution, the model decides whether or not to move its eyes (and if so where to move them to) and the cycle repeats.

3.1 Formal problem of reading: Actions

The model assumes that on each of a series of discrete timesteps, the model obtains visual input around the current location of the eyes, and then chooses between three actions: (a) continuing to fixate the currently fixated position, (b) initiating a saccade to a new position, or (c) stopping reading. If the model chooses option (a), time simply advances, and if it chooses option (c), then reading immediately ends. If a saccade is initiated (b), there is a lag of two timesteps, representing the time required to plan and execute a saccade, during which the model again obtains visual input around the current position, and then the eyes move toward the intended target. Because of motor error, the actual landing position of the eyes is normally distributed around the intended target with the standard deviation in characters given by a linear function of the intended distance d ($.87 + .084d$; Engbert et al., 2005).[1]

3.2 Language knowledge

Following Bicknell and Levy (2010), we use very simple probabilistic models of language knowledge: word n-gram models (Jurafsky & Martin, 2009), which encode the probability of each word conditional on the $n-1$ previous words.

3.3 Formal model of visual input

Visual input in the model consists of noisy information about the positions and identities of the characters in the text. Crucially, in this extended version of the model, this includes noisy information about the length of words. We begin with a visual acuity function taken from Engbert et al. (2005). This function decreases exponentially with retinal eccentricity ε, and decreases asymmetrically, falling off more slowly to the right than the left.[2] The model obtains visual input from the 19 character positions with the highest acuity $\varepsilon \in [-7, 12]$, which we refer to as the perceptual span. In order to provide the model with information about the current fixation position within the text, the model also obtains veridical information about the number of word boundaries to the left of the perceptual span.

Visual information from the perceptual span consists of stochastic information about the number of characters in the region and their identities. We make the simplifying assumption that the only characters are letters and spaces. Formally, visual input on a given timestep is represented as a string of symbols, each element of which has two features. One feature denotes whether the symbol represents a space ([+SPACE]) or a letter ([−SPACE]), an important distinction because spaces indicate word boundaries. Symbols that are [+SPACE] veridically indicate the occurrence of a space, while [−SPACE] symbols provide noisy information about the letter's identity. The other feature attached to each symbol specifies whether the character in the text that the symbol was emitted from was being fixated ([+FIX]) or not ([−FIX]). The centrally fixated character has special status so that the model can recover the eyes' position within the visual span.

This visual input string is generated by a process of moving a marker from the beginning to the end of the perceptual span, generally inserting a symbol into the visual input string for each character it moves across (EMISSION). To provide only noisy information about word length, however, this process is not always one of EMISSION, but sometimes it inserts a symbol into the visual input string that does not correspond to a character in the text (INSERTION), and at other times it fails to insert a symbol for a character in the text (SKIPPING). Specifically, at each step of the process, a decision is first made about INSERTION, which occurs with probability δ. If INSERTION occurs, then a [−SPACE] identity for the character is chosen according to a uniform distribution, and then noisy visual information about that character is generated in the same way as for EMISSION (described below). If a character is not inserted, and the marker has already moved past the last character in the perceptual span, the process terminates. Otherwise, a decision is made about whether to emit a symbol into the visual input string from the character at the marker's current position (EMISSION) or whether to skip outputting a symbol for that character (SKIPPING). In either case, the marker is advanced to the next character position. If the character at the marker's cur-

[1] In the terminology of the literature, the model has only random motor error (variance), not systematic error (bias). Following Engbert and Krügel (2010), systematic error may arise from Bayesian estimation of the best saccade distance.

[2] While we refer to this function as visual acuity, it is clear from its asymmetric nature that it has an attentional component.

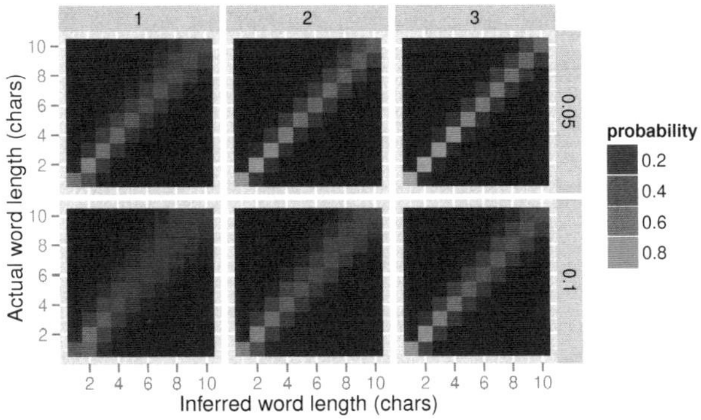

Figure 1: The expectation for the posterior distribution over the length of a word for actual lengths 1–10 after the model has received 1, 2, or 3 timesteps of visual input about the word, for two levels of length uncertainty: $\delta \in \{.05, .1\}$. These calculations use as a prior distribution the empirical distribution of word length in the BNC and assume no information about letter identity.

rent position is $[+\text{SPACE}]$ or $[+\text{FIX}]$, then EMISSION is always chosen, but if it is any other character, then SKIPPING occurs with probability δ.

A $[-\text{SPACE}]$ symbol (produced through EMISSION or INSERTION) contains noisy information about the identity of the letter that generated it, obtained via sampling. Specifically, we represent each letter as a 26-dimensional vector, where a single element is 1 and the others are zeros. Given this representation, a $[-\text{SPACE}]$ symbol contains a sample from a 26-dimensional Gaussian with a mean equal to the letter's true identity and a diagonal covariance matrix $\Sigma(\varepsilon) = \lambda(\varepsilon)^{-1}I$, where $\lambda(\varepsilon)$ is the visual acuity at eccentricity ε. We scale the overall processing rate by multiplying each rate by Λ, set to 8 for the simulations reported here.

Allowing for INSERTION and SKIPPING means that visual input yields noisy information about the length of words, and this noise is such that uncertainty is higher for longer words. Figure 1 gives a visualization of this uncertainty. It shows the expectation for the posterior distribution over the length of a word for a range of actual word lengths, after the model has received 1, 2, or 3 timesteps of visual input about the word, at two levels of uncertainty. This figure demonstrates two things: first, that there is substantial uncertainty about word length even after three timesteps of visual input, and second, that this uncertainty is larger for longer words.

(a)	$m = [.6, .7, \mathbf{.6}, .4, .3, .6]$:	Keep fixating (3)
(b)	$m = [.6, .4, \mathbf{.9}, .4, .3, .6]$:	Move back (to 2)
(c)	$m = [.6, .7, \mathbf{.9}, .4, .3, .6]$:	Move forward (to 6)
(d)	$m = [.6, .7, \mathbf{.9}, .8, .7, .7]$:	Stop reading

Figure 2: Values of m for a 6 character text under which a model fixating position 3 would take each of its four actions, if $\alpha = .7$ and $\beta = .5$.

3.4 Inference about text identity

The model's initial beliefs about the identity of the text are given by the probability of each possible identity under the language model. On each timestep, the model obtains a visual input string as described above and calculates the likelihood of generating that string from each possible identity of the text. The model then updates its beliefs about the text via standard Bayesian inference: multiplying the probability of each text identity under its prior beliefs by the likelihood of generating the visual input string from that text identity and normalizing. We compactly represent all of these distributions using weighted finite-state transducers (Mohri, 1997) using the OpenFST library (Allauzen, Riley, Schalkwyk, Skut, & Mohri, 2007), and implement belief update with transducer composition and weight pushing.

3.5 Behavior policy

The model uses a simple policy with two parameters, α and β, to decide between actions based on the marginal probability m of the most likely character c in each position j,

$$m(j) = \max_{c} p(w_j = c)$$

where w_j indicates the character in the jth position. A high value of m indicates relative confidence about the character's identity, and a low value relative uncertainty. Because our extension has uncertainty about the absolute position of its eyes within the text, each position j is now defined relative to the centrally fixated character.

Figure 2 illustrates how the model decides among four possible actions. If the value of $m(j)$ for the current position of the eyes is less than the parameter α, the model continues fixating the current position (2a). Otherwise, if the value of $m(j)$ is less than the parameter β for some leftward position, the model initiates a saccade to the closest such position (2b). If no such positions exist to the left, the model initiates a saccade to n characters past the closest position to the right for which $m(j) < \alpha$ (2c).[3] Finally, if no such positions exist, the model stops reading (2d). Intuitively, then, the model reads by making a rightward sweep to bring its confidence in each character up to α, but pauses to move left to reread any character whose confidence falls below β.

4 Simulation 1: full model

We now assess the effects of word length produced by the extended version of the model. Following Bicknell (2011), we use the model to simulate reading of a modified version of the Schilling, Rayner, and Chumbley (1998) corpus of typical sentences used in reading experiments. We compare three levels of length uncertainty: $\delta \in \{0, .05, .1\}$. The first of these ($\delta = 0$) corresponds to Bicknell and Levy's (2010) model, which has no uncertainty about word length. We predict that increasing the amount of length uncertainty will make effects of word length more like those of humans, and we compare the model's length effects to those of human readers of the Schilling corpus.

4.1 Methods

4.1.1 Model parameters and language model

Following Bicknell (2011), the model's language knowledge was an unsmoothed bigram model using a vocabulary set consisting of the 500 most frequent words in the British National Corpus (BNC) as well as all the words in the test corpus. Every bigram in the BNC was counted for which both words were in vocabulary, and – due to the intense computation required for exact inference – this set was trimmed by removing rare bigrams that occur less than 200 times (except for bigrams that occur in the test corpus), resulting in a set of about 19,000 bigrams, from which the bigram model was constructed.

4.1.2 Optimization of policy parameters

We set the parameters of the behavior policy (α, β) to values that maximize reading efficiency. We define reading efficiency E to be an interpolation of speed and accuracy, $E = (1-\gamma)L - \gamma T$, where L is the log probability of the true identity of the text under the model's beliefs at the end of reading, T is the number of timesteps before the model stopped reading, and γ gives the relative value of speed. For the present simulations, we use $\gamma = .1$, which produces reasonably accurate reading. To find optimal values of the policy parameters α and β for each model, we use the PEGASUS method (Ng & Jordan, 2000) to transform this stochastic optimization problem into a deterministic one amenable to standard optimization algorithms, and then use coordinate ascent.

4.1.3 Test corpus

We test the model on a corpus of 33 sentences from the Schilling corpus slightly modified by Bicknell and Levy (2010) so that every bigram occurred in the BNC, ensuring that the results do not depend on smoothing.

4.1.4 Analysis

With each model, we performed 50 stochastic simulations of the reading of the corpus. For each run, we calculated the four standard eye movement measures mentioned above for each word in the corpus: first fixation duration, gaze duration, skipping probability, and refixation probability. We then averaged each of these four measures across runs for each word token in the corpus, yielding a single mean value for each measure for each word.

Comparing the fixation duration measures to humans required converting the model's timesteps into milliseconds. We performed this scaling by multiplying the duration of each fixation by a conversion factor set to be equal to the mean human gaze duration divided by the mean model gaze duration for words with frequencies higher than 1 in 100, meaning that the model predictions exactly match the human mean for gaze durations on these words.

4.2 Results

Figure 3 presents the results for all four measures of interest. Looking first at the model with no uncertainty, we see that the results replicate those of Bicknell (2011): while there is a monotonic effect of word length on skip rates and refixation rates in the same direction as humans, longer words receive

[3] The role of n is to ensure that the model does not center its visual field on the first uncertain character. For the present simulations, we did not optimize this parameter, but fixed $n = 3$.

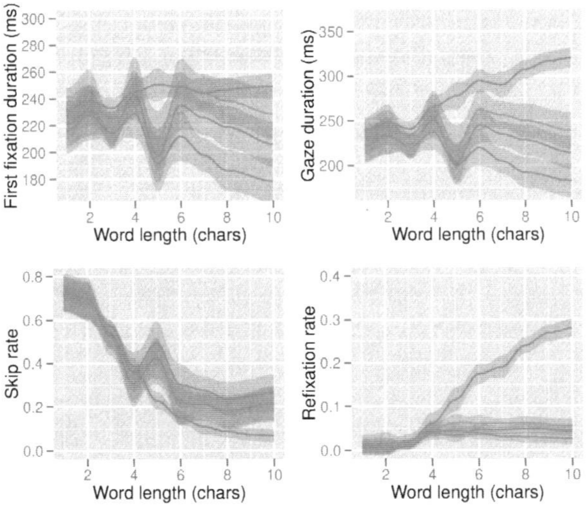

Figure 3: Effects of word length in three version of the full model with $\delta = 0$ (red), $\delta = 0.05$ (green), and $\delta = 0.1$ (blue) on first fixation durations, gaze durations, skip rates, and refixation rates compared with the empirical human data for this corpus (purple). Estimates obtained via loess smoothing and plotted with standard errors.

shorter fixations in the model, opposite to the pattern found in human data. As predicted, adding length uncertainty begins to reverse this effect: as uncertainty is increased, the effect of word length on fixation durations becomes less negative.

However, while these results look more like those of humans, there are still substantial differences. For one, even for the model with the most uncertainty, the effect of word length – while not negative – is also not really positive. Second, the effect appears rather non-monotonic. We hypothesize that these two problems are related to the aggressive trimming we performed of the model's language model. By removing low frequency words and bigrams, we artificially trimmed especially the visual neighborhoods of long words, since frequency and length are negatively correlated. This could have led to another inverse word length effect, which even adding more length uncertainty was unable to fully overcome. In effect, extending the visual neighborhoods of long words (by adding length uncertainty) may not have much effect if we have removed all the words that would be in those extended neighborhoods. In addition, the aggressive trimming could have been responsible for the non-monotonicities apparent in the model's predictions. We performed another set of simulations using a language model with substantially less trimming to test these hypotheses.

5 Simulation 2: model without context

In this simulation, we used a unigram language model instead of the bigram language model used in Simulation 1. Since this model cannot make use of linguistic context, it will not show as robust effects of linguistic variables such as word predictability (Bicknell & Levy, 2012), but since here our focus is on effects of word length, this limitation is unlikely to concern us. Crucially, because of the model's simpler structure, it allows for the use of a substantially larger vocabulary than the bigram model used in Simulation 1. In addition, using this model avoids the problems mentioned above associated with trimming bigrams. We predicted that this language model would allow us to obtain effects of word length on fixation durations that were actually positive (rather than merely non-negative), and that there would be fewer non-monotonicities in the function.

5.1 Methods

Except the following, the methods were identical to those of Simulation 1. We replaced the bigram language model with a unigram language model. Training was performed in the same manner, except that instead of including only the most common 500 words in the BNC, we included all words that occur at least 200 times (corresponding to a frequency of 2 per million; about 19,000 words). Because of the greater computational complexity for the two models with non-zero δ, we performed only 20 simulations of the reading of the corpus instead of 50.

5.2 Results

Figure 4 presents the results for all four measures of interest. Looking at the model with no uncertainty, we see already that the predictions are a substantially better fit to human data than was the full model. The skipping and refixation rates look substantially more like the human curves. And while the word length effect on first fixation duration is still negative, it is already non-negative for gaze duration. This supports our hypotheses that aggressive trimming were partly responsible for the full model's negative word length effect.

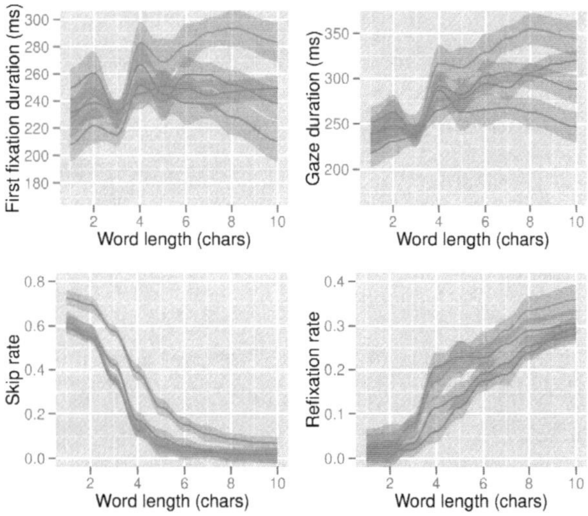

Figure 4: Effects of word length in three version of the model without context (unigram model) with $\delta = 0$ (red), $\delta = 0.05$ (green), and $\delta = 0.1$ (blue) on first fixation durations, gaze durations, skip rates, and refixation rates compared with the empirical human data for this corpus (purple). Estimates obtained via loess smoothing and plotted with standard errors.

Moving on to the models with uncertainty, we see that predictions are still in good agreement with humans for skip rates and refixation rates. More interestingly, we see that adding length uncertainty makes both durations measures relatively positive functions of word length. While the overall size of the effect is incorrect for first fixation durations, we see striking similarities between the models predictions and human data on both duration measures. For first fixations, the human pattern is that durations go up from word lengths 1 to 2, down from 2 to 3 (presumably because of 'the'), and then up to 5, after which the function is relatively flat. That pattern also holds for both models with uncertainty. For gaze duration, both models more or less reproduce the human pattern of a steadily-increasing function throughout the range, and again match the human function in dipping for word length 3. For gaze durations, even the overall size of the effect produced by the model is similar to that of humans. These results confirm our original hypothesis that adding length uncertainty would lead to more humanlike word length effects. In addition, comparing the results of Simulation 2 with Simulation 1 reveals the importance to this account of words having realistic visual neighborhoods. When the visual neighborhoods of (especially longer) words were trimmed to be artificially sparse, adding length uncertainty did not allow the model to recover the human pattern.

6 Conclusion

In this paper, we argued that the success of major models of eye movements in reading to reproduce the (positive) human effect of word length via acuity limitations may be a result of not including opposing factors such as the negative correlation between visual neighborhood size and word length. We described the failure of the rational model presented in Bicknell and Levy (2010) to obtain humanlike effects of word length, despite including all of these factors, suggesting that our understanding of word length effects in reading is incomplete. We proposed a new reason for word length effects – uncertainty about word length that is larger for longer words – and noted that this reason was not implemented in Bicknell and Levy's model because of a simplifying assumption. We presented an extension of the model relaxing this assumption, in which readers obtain noisy information about word length, and showed through two sets of simulations that the new model produces effects of word length that look more like those of human readers. Interestingly, while adding length uncertainty made both models more humanlike, it was only in Simulation 2 – in which words had more realistic visual neighborhoods – that all measures of the effect of word length on eye movements showed the human pattern, underscoring the importance of the structure of the language for this account of word length effects.

We take these results as evidence that word length effects cannot be completely explained through limitations on visual acuity. Rather, they suggest that a full understanding of the reasons underlying word length effects on eye movements in reading should include a notion of uncertainty about the number of letters in a word, which grows with word length.

Acknowledgments

This research was supported by NIH grant T32-DC000041 from the Center for Research in Language at UC San Diego to K. B. and by NSF grant 0953870 and NIH grant R01-HD065829 to R. L.

References

Allauzen, C., Riley, M., Schalkwyk, J., Skut, W., & Mohri, M. (2007). OpenFst: A general and efficient weighted finite-state transducer library. In *Proceedings of the Ninth International Conference on Implementation and Application of Automata, (CIAA 2007)* (Vol. 4783, p. 11-23). Springer.

Balota, D. A., Cortese, M. J., Sergent-Marshall, S. D., Spieler, D. H., & Yap, M. J. (2004). Visual word recognition of single-syllable words. *Journal of Experimental Psychology: General*, *133*, 283–316.

Bicknell, K. (2011). *Eye movements in reading as rational behavior*. Unpublished doctoral dissertation, University of California, San Diego.

Bicknell, K., & Levy, R. (2010). A rational model of eye movement control in reading. In *Proceedings of the 48th Annual Meeting of the Association for Computational Linguistics (ACL)* (pp. 1168–1178). Uppsala, Sweden: Association for Computational Linguistics.

Bicknell, K., & Levy, R. (2012). Word predictability and frequency effects in a rational model of reading. In N. Miyake, D. Peebles, & R. P. Cooper (Eds.), *Proceedings of the 34th Annual Conference of the Cognitive Science Society.* Austin, TX: Cognitive Science Society.

Bicknell, K., & Levy, R. (in press). The utility of modelling word identification from visual input within models of eye movements in reading. *Visual Cognition*.

Dehaene, S. (1997). *The number sense: How the mind creates mathematics*. New York: Oxford University Press.

Engbert, R., & Krügel, A. (2010). Readers use Bayesian estimation for eye movement control. *Psychological Science*, *21*, 366–371.

Engbert, R., Longtin, A., & Kliegl, R. (2002). A dynamical model of saccade generation in reading based on spatially distributed lexical processing. *Vision Research*, *42*, 621–636.

Engbert, R., Nuthmann, A., Richter, E. M., & Kliegl, R. (2005). SWIFT: A dynamical model of saccade generation during reading. *Psychological Review*, *112*, 777–813.

Gomez, P., Ratcliff, R., & Perea, M. (2008). The Overlap model: A model of letter position coding. *Psychological Review*, *115*, 577–601.

Grainger, J., Granier, J.-P., Farioli, F., Van Assche, E., & van Heuven, W. J. B. (2006). Letter position information and printed word perception: The relative-position priming constraint. *Journal of Experimental Psychology: Human Perception and Performance*, *32*, 865–884.

Jurafsky, D., & Martin, J. H. (2009). *Speech and language processing: An introduction to natural language processing, computational linguistics, and speech recognition* (2nd ed.). Upper Saddle River, NJ: Prentice Hall.

Mohri, M. (1997). Finite-state transducers in language and speech processing. *Computational Linguistics*, *23*, 269–311.

Ng, A. Y., & Jordan, M. (2000). PEGASUS: A policy search method for large MDPs and POMDPs. In *Uncertainty in Artificial Intelligence, Proceedings of the Sixteenth Conference* (pp. 406–415).

Norris, D., Kinoshita, S., & van Casteren, M. (2010). A stimulus sampling theory of letter identity and order. *Journal of Memory and Language*, *62*, 254–271.

Peressotti, F., & Grainger, J. (1999). The role of letter identity and letter position in orthographic priming. *Perception & Psychophysics*, *61*, 691–706.

Pollatsek, A., Perea, M., & Binder, K. S. (1999). The effects of "neighborhood size" in reading and lexical decision. *Journal of Experimental Psychology: Human Perception and Performance*, *25*, 1142–1158.

Pollatsek, A., Reichle, E. D., & Rayner, K. (2006). Tests of the E-Z Reader model: Exploring the interface between cognition and eye-movement control. *Cognitive Psychology*, *52*, 1–56.

Reichle, E. D., Pollatsek, A., Fisher, D. L., & Rayner, K. (1998). Toward a model of eye movement control in reading. *Psychological Review*, *105*, 125–157.

Reichle, E. D., Rayner, K., & Pollatsek, A. (2003). The E-Z Reader model of cye-movement control in reading: Comparisons to other models.

Behavioral and Brain Sciences, *26*, 445–526.

Schilling, H. E. H., Rayner, K., & Chumbley, J. I. (1998). Comparing naming, lexical decision, and eye fixation times: Word frequency effects and individual differences. *Memory & Cognition*, *26*, 1270–1281.

Yarkoni, T., Balota, D. A., & Yap, M. J. (2008). Moving beyond Coltheart's N: A new measure of orthographic similarity. *Psychonomic Bulletin & Review*, *15*, 971–979.

Minimal Dependency Length in Realization Ranking

Michael White and **Rajakrishnan Rajkumar**
Department of Linguistics
The Ohio State University
Columbus, OH, USA
{mwhite,raja}@ling.osu.edu

Abstract

Comprehension and corpus studies have found that the tendency to minimize dependency length has a strong influence on constituent ordering choices. In this paper, we investigate dependency length minimization in the context of discriminative realization ranking, focusing on its potential to eliminate egregious ordering errors as well as better match the distributional characteristics of sentence orderings in news text. We find that with a state-of-the-art, comprehensive realization ranking model, dependency length minimization yields statistically significant improvements in BLEU scores and significantly reduces the number of heavy/light ordering errors. Through distributional analyses, we also show that with simpler ranking models, dependency length minimization can go overboard, too often sacrificing canonical word order to shorten dependencies, while richer models manage to better counterbalance the dependency length minimization preference against (sometimes) competing canonical word order preferences.

1 Introduction

In this paper, we show that for the constituent ordering problem in surface realization, incorporating insights from the minimal dependency length theory of language production (Temperley, 2007) into a discriminative realization ranking model yields significant improvements upon a state-of-the-art baseline. We demonstrate empirically using OpenCCG, our CCG-based (Steedman, 2000) surface realization system, the utility of a global feature encoding the total dependency length of a given derivation. Although other works in the realization literature have used head-dependent distances in their models (Filippova and Strube, 2009; Velldal and Oepen, 2005; White and Rajkumar, 2009), to the best of our knowledge, this paper is the first to use insights from the minimal dependency theory directly and study their effects, both qualitatively and quantitatively.

Table 1 shows examples of how the dependency length feature affects the output in comparison to a model with a rich set of discriminative syntactic and dependency ordering features, but no features directly targeting relative weight (see Table 3 for model details). In wsj_0015.7, the dependency length models produce an exact match, while the DEPORD model fails to shift the short temporal adverbial *next year* next to the verb, leaving a confusingly repetitive *this year next year* at the end of the sentence. In wsj_0020.1, the dependency length models produce a nearly exact match with just an equally acceptable inversion of *closely watching*. By contrast, the DEPORD model mistakenly shifts the direct object *South Korea, Taiwan and Saudia Arabia* to the end of the sentence where it is difficult to understand following two very long intervening phrases. In wsj_0021.8, all the models mysteriously put *not* in front of the auxiliary and leave out the complementizer, but DEPORD also mistakenly leaves *before* at the end of the verb phrase where it is again apt to be interpreted as modifying the preceding verb. Finally, wsj_0014.2 shows a case where DEPORD is nearly an exact match (except for a missing comma) but the dependency length models front the PP *on the 12-member board*, where it is gram-

wsj_0015.7	the exact amount of the refund will be determined **next year** based on actual collections made until Dec. 31 of this year .
DEPLEN	[same]
DEPORD	the exact amount of the refund will be determined based on actual collections made until Dec. 31 of this year *next year* .
wsj_0020.1	the U.S. , claiming some success in its trade diplomacy , removed South Korea , Taiwan and Saudi Arabia from a list of countries it is closely watching for allegedly failing to honor U.S. patents , copyrights and other intellectual-property rights .
DEPLEN	the U.S. , claiming some success in its trade diplomacy , removed **South Korea , Taiwan and Saudi Arabia** from a list of countries it is *watching closely* for allegedly failing to honor U.S. patents , copyrights and other intellectual-property rights .
DEPORD	the U.S. removed from a list of countries it is *watching closely* for allegedly failing to honor U.S. patents , copyrights and other intellectual-property rights , claiming some success in its trade diplomacy , *South Korea , Taiwan and Saudi Arabia* .
wsj_0021.8	but he has not said before that the country wants half the debt forgiven .
DEPLEN	but he *not* has said **before** $\emptyset$ the country wants half the debt forgiven .
DEPORD	but he *not* has said $\emptyset$ the country wants half the debt forgiven **before** .
wsj_0014.2	they succeed Daniel M. Rexinger , retired Circuit City executive vice president , and Robert R. Glauber , U.S. Treasury undersecretary , on the 12-member board .
DEPORD	they succeed Daniel M. Rexinger , retired Circuit City executive vice president , and Robert R. Glauber , U.S. Treasury undersecretary $\emptyset$ on the 12-member board .
DEPLEN	*on the 12-member board* they succeed Daniel M. Rexinger , retired Circuit City executive vice president , and Robert R. Glauber , U.S. Treasury undersecretary .
wsj_0075.13 DEPORD, DEPLEN	The Treasury also said it plans to sell [$ 10 billion] [in 36-day cash management bills] [on Thursday].
Temperley (p.c.)	[In 1976], [as a film student at the Purchase campus of the State University of New York], Mr. Lane, shot ...

Table 1: Examples of Realized Output for Models with and without Dependency Length Feature (see Table 3 for model details)

matical but rather marked (and not motivated in the discourse context).

Cases like the final example above point to the fact that dependency length is more of a preference than an optimization objective, which must be balanced against other order preferences at times. A closer reading of Temperley's (2007) study reveals that dependency length can sometimes run counter to many canonical word order choices. A case in point is the class of examples involving pre-modifying adjunct sequences that precede both the subject and the verb. Assuming that their parent head is the main verb of the sentence, a long-short sequence would minimize overall dependency length. However, in 613 examples found in the Penn Treebank, the average length of the first adjunct was 3.15 words while the second adjunct was 3.48 words long, thus reflecting a short-long pattern (illustrated in the Temperley p.c. example). Apart from these, Hawkins (2001) shows that arguments are generally located closer to the verb than adjuncts. Gildea and Temperley (2007) also suggest that adverb placement might involve cases which go against dependency length minimization. An examination of 295 legitimate long-short post-verbal constituent orders (counter to dependency length) from Section 00 of the Penn Treebank revealed that temporal adverb phrases are often involved in long-short orders, as shown in wsj_0075.13 in Table 1. In our setup, the preference to minimize dependency length can be balanced by features capturing preferences for alternate choices (e.g. the argument-adjunct distinction in the dependency ordering model). Via distributional analyses, we show that while simpler realization ranking models can go overboard in minimizing dependency length, richer models largely succeed in overcoming this issue, while still taking advantage of dependency length minimization to avoid egregious ordering errors.

2 Background

2.1 Minimal Dependency Length

Comprehension and corpus studies (Gibson, 1998; Gibson, 2000; Temperley, 2007) point to the tendency of production and comprehension systems to adhere to principles of dependency length minimization. The idea of dependency length minimization is based on Gibson's (1998) Dependency Locality Theory (DLT) of comprehension, which predicts that longer dependencies are more difficult to process. DLT predictions have been further validated using comprehension studies involving eye-tracking corpora (Demberg and Keller, 2008). DLT metrics also correlate reasonably well with activation decay over time expressed in computational models of comprehension (Lewis et al., 2006; Lewis and Vasishth, 2005).

Extending these ideas from comprehension, Temperley (2007) poses the question: Does language production reflect a preference for shorter dependencies as well so as to facilitate comprehension? By means of a study of Penn Treebank data, Temperley shows that English sentences do display a tendency to minimize the sum of all their head-dependent distances as illustrated by a variety of constructions. Further, Gildea and Temperley (2007) report that random linearizations have higher dependency lengths compared to actual English, while an "optimal" algorithm (from the perspective of dependency length minimization), which places dependents on either sides of a head in order of increasing length, is closer to actual English. Tily (2010) also applies insights from the above cited papers to show that dependency length constitutes a significant pressure towards language change. For head-final languages, dependency length minimization results in the "long-short" constituent ordering in language production (Yamashita and Chang, 2001). More generally, Hawkins's (1994; 2000) processing domains, dependency length minimization and end-weight effects in constituent ordering (Wasow and Arnold, 2003) are all very closely related. The dependency length hypothesis goes beyond the predictions made by Hawkins' *Minimize Domains* principle in the case of English clauses with three post-verbal adjuncts: Gibson's DLT correctly predicts that the first constituent tends to be shorter than the second, while Hawkins' approach does not make predictions about the relative orders of the first two constituents.

However, it would be very reductive to consider dependency length minimization as the sole factor in language production. In fact, a large body of prior work discusses a variety of other factors involved in language production. These other preferences are either correlated with dependency length or can override the minimal dependency length preference. Complexity (Wasow, 2002; Wasow and Arnold, 2003), animacy (Snider and Zaenen, 2006; Branigan et al., 2008), information status considerations (Wasow and Arnold, 2003; Arnold et al., 2000), the argument-adjunct distinction (Hawkins, 2001) and lexical bias (Wasow and Arnold, 2003; Bresnan et al., 2007) are a few prominent factors. More recently, Anttila et al. (2010) argued that the principle of end weight can be revised by calculating weight in prosodic terms to provide more explanatory power. As Temperley (2007) suggests, a satisfactory model should combine insights from multiple approaches, a theme which we investigate in this work by means of a rich feature set adapted from the parsing and realization literature. Our feature design has been inspired by the conclusions of the above-cited works pertaining to the role of dependency length minimization in syntactic choice in conjuction with other factors influencing constituent order. However, going beyond Temperley's corpus study, we confirm the utility of incorporating a feature for minimizing dependency length into machine-learned models with hundreds of thousands of features found to be useful in previous parsing and realization work, and investigate the extent to which these features can counterbalance a dependency length minimization preference in cases where canonical word order considerations should prevail.

2.2 Surface Realization with Combinatory Categorial Grammar (CCG)

CCG (Steedman, 2000) is a unification-based categorial grammar formalism defined almost entirely in terms of lexical entries that encode subcategorization as well as syntactic features (e.g. number and agreement). OpenCCG is a parsing/generation library which includes a hybrid symbolic-statistical chart realizer (White, 2006). The input to the OpenCCG realizer is a semantic graph, where each node has a lexical predication and a set of semantic features; nodes are connected via dependency relations. Internally, such graphs are represented using Hybrid Logic Dependency Semantics (HLDS), a dependency-based approach to representing linguistic meaning (Baldridge and Kruijff, 2002). Alternative realizations are ranked using integrated n-gram or averaged perceptron scoring models. In the experiments reported below, the inputs are derived from the gold standard derivations in the CCGbank (Hockenmaier and Steedman, 2007), and the outputs are the highest-scoring realizations found during the realizer's chart-based search.[1]

3 Feature Design

In the realm of paraphrasing using tree linearization, Kempen and Harbusch (2004) explore features which have later been appropriated into classification approaches for surface realization (Filippova and Strube, 2007). Prominent features include information status, animacy and phrase length. In the case of ranking models for surface realization, by far the most comprehensive experiments involving linguistically motivated features are reported in work of Cahill for German realization ranking (Cahill et al., 2007; Cahill and Riester, 2009). Apart from language model and Lexical Functional Grammar (LFG) c-structure and f-structure based features, Cahill also designed and incorporated features modeling information status considerations.

The feature sets explored in this paper extend those in previous work on realization ranking with OpenCCG using averaged perceptron models (White and Rajkumar, 2009; Rajkumar et al., 2009; Rajkumar and White, 2010) to include more comprehensive ordering features. The feature classes are listed below, where DEPLEN, HOCKENMAIER and DEPORD are novel, and the rest are as in earlier OpenCCG models. The inclusion of the DEPORD features is intended to yield a model with a similarly rich set of ordering features as Cahill and Forster's (2009) realization ranking model for German.

DEPLEN The total of the length between all heads and dependents for a realization, where length is in intervening words[2] excluding punctuation. For length purposes, collapsed named entities were counted as a single word in the experiments reported here.

NGRAMS The log probabilities of the word sequence scored using three different n-gram models: a trigram word model, a trigram word model with named entity classes replacing words, and a trigram model over POS tags and supertags.

HOCKENMAIER As an extra component of the generative baseline, a reimplementation of Hockenmaier's (2003) generative syntactic model.

DISCRIMINATIVE NGRAMS Sequences from each of the n-gram models as indicator features in the perceptron model.

AGREEMENT Indicator features for subject-verb and animacy agreement as well as balanced punctuation.

C&C NF BASE The features from Clark & Curran's (2007) normal form model, minus the distance features.

C&C NF DISTANCE The distance features from the C&C normal form model.

[1]The realizer can also be run using inputs derived from OpenCCG's parser, though informal experiments suggest that parse errors tend to decrease generation quality.

[2]We also experimented with two other definitions of dependency length described in the literature, namely (1) counting only nouns and verbs to approximate counting by discourse referents (Gibson, 1998) and (2) omitting function words to approximate prosodic weight (Anttila et al., 2010); however, realization ranking accuracy was slightly worse than counting all non-punctuation words.

Feature Type	Example
HeadBroadPos + Rel + Precedes + HeadWord + DepWord	⟨VB, Arg0, dep, wants, he⟩
... + HeadWord + DepPOS	⟨VB, Arg0, dep, wants, PRP⟩
... + HeadPOS + DepWord	⟨VB, Arg0, dep, VBZ, he⟩
... + HeadWord + DepPOS	⟨VB, Arg0, dep, VBZ, PRP⟩
HeadBroadPos + Side + DepWord1 + DepWord2	⟨NN, left, an, important⟩
... + DepWord1 + DepPOS2	⟨NN, left, an, JJ⟩
... + DepPOS1 + DepWord2	⟨NN, left, DT, important⟩
... + DepPOS1 + DepPOS2	⟨NN, left, DT, JJ⟩
... + Rel1 + Rel2	⟨NN, left, Det, Mod⟩

Table 2: Basic head-dependent and sibling dependent ordering features

DEPORD Several classes of features for ordering heads and dependents as well as sibling dependents on the same side of the head. The basic features—using words, POS tags and dependency relations, grouped by the broad POS tag of the head—are shown in Table 2. There are also similar features using words and a word class (instead of words and POS tags), where the class is either the named entity class, COLOR for color words, PRO for pronouns, one of 60-odd suffixes culled from the web, or HYPHEN or CAP for hyphenated or capitalized words. Additionally, there are features for detecting definiteness of an NP or PP (where the definiteness value is used in place of the POS tag).

4 Evaluation

4.1 Experimental Conditions

We followed the averaged perceptron training procedure of White and Rajkumar (2009) with a couple of updates. First, as noted earlier, we used a reimplementation of Hockenmaier's (2003) generative syntactic model as an extra component of our generative baseline; and second, only five epochs of training were used, which was found to work as well as using additional epochs on the development set. As in the earlier work, the models were trained on the standard training sections (02–21) of an enhanced version of the CCGbank, using a lexico-grammar extracted from these sections.

The models tested in the experiments reported below are summarized in Table 3. The three groups of models are designed to test the impact of the dependency length feature when added to feature sets of increasing complexity. In more detail, the GLOBAL and DEPLEN-GLOBAL models contain dense features on entire derivations; their values are the log probabilities of the three n-gram models used in the earlier work along with the Hockenmaier model (and the dependency length feature, in DEPLEN-GLOBAL). The second group is centered on DEPORD-NODIST, which contains all features except the dependency length feature and the distance features in Clark & Curran's normal form model, which may indirectly capture some dependency length minimization preferences (365,287 features in all). In addition to DEPLEN-NODIST (366,094 features)—where the dependency length feature is added—this group also contains DEPORD-NONF (269,249), which is designed to test (as a side comparison) whether the Clark & Curran normal form base features are still useful even when used in conjunction with the new dependency ordering features. In the final group, DEPORD-NF contains all the 431,226 features examined in this paper except the dependency length feature, while DEPLEN contains all the features including the dependency length feature (total 428,775 features). Note that the weight of the total dependency length feature was negative in each case, as expected.

4.2 BLEU Results

Following the usual practice in the realization ranking, we evaluate our results quantitatively using exact matches and BLEU (Papineni et al., 2002), a corpus similarity metric developed for MT evaluation. Realization results for the development and test sections appear in Table 4. For all three model groups, the dependency length feature yields significant increases in BLEU scores, even in comparison to the

Model	Dep Len	Ngram Mods	Hocken-maier	Discr Ngrams	Agree-ment	C&C NF Base	C&C NF Dist	Dep Ord
GLOBAL	N	Y	Y	N	N	N	N	N
DEPLEN-GLOBAL	Y	Y	Y	N	N	N	N	N
DEPORD-NONF	N	Y	Y	Y	Y	N	N	Y
DEPORD-NODIST	N	Y	Y	Y	Y	Y	N	Y
DEPLEN-NODIST	Y	Y	Y	Y	Y	Y	N	Y
DEPORD-NF	N	Y	Y	Y	Y	Y	Y	Y
DEPLEN	Y	Y	Y	Y	Y	Y	Y	Y

Table 3: Legend for Experimental Conditions

Model	% Exact	BLEU	Signif
Sect 00			
GLOBAL	33.03	0.8292	-
DEPLEN-GLOBAL	34.73	**0.8345**	***
DEPORD-NONF	42.33	0.8534	**
DEPORD-NODIST	43.12	0.8560	-
DEPLEN-NODIST	43.87	**0.8587**	***
DEPORD-NF	43.44	0.8590	-
DEPLEN	44.56	**0.8610**	**
Sect 23			
GLOBAL	34.75	0.8302	-
DEPLEN-GLOBAL	34.70	**0.8330**	***
DEPORD-NODIST	41.42	0.8561	-
DEPLEN-NODIST	42.95	**0.8603**	***
DEPORD-NF	41.32	0.8577	-
DEPLEN	42.05	**0.8596**	**

Table 4: Development (Section 00) & Test (Section 23) Set Results—exact match percentage and BLEU scores, along with statistical significance of BLEU compared to the unmarked model in each group (* = $p < 0.1$, ** = $p < 0.05$, *** = $p < 0.01$); significant within-group winners (at $p < 0.05$) are shown in bold

model (DEPORD-NF) containing Clark & Curran's distance features in addition to the new dependency ordering features (as well as all other features but total dependency length). The second group additionally shows that the Clark & Curran normal form base features do indeed have a significant impact on BLEU scores even when used with the new dependency ordering model, as DEPORD-NONF is significantly worse than DEPORD-NODIST (the impact of the distance features is evident in the increases from the second group to the third group). As with the dev set, the dependency length feature yielded a significant increase in BLEU scores for each comparison on the test set also.

For each group, the statistical significance of the difference in BLEU scores between a model and the unmarked model (-) is determined by bootstrap resampling (Koehn, 2004).[3] Note that although the differences in BLEU scores are small, they end up being statistically significant because the models frequently yield the same top scoring realization, and reliably deliver improvements in the cases where they differ. In particular, note that DEPLEN and DEPORD-NF agree on the best realization 81% of the time, while DEPLEN-NODIST and DEPORD-NODIST have 78.1% agreement, and DEPLEN-GLOBAL and GLOBAL show 77.4% agreement; by comparison, DEPORD-NODIST and GLOBAL only agree on the best realization 51.1% of the time. With exact matches, the dependency length feature increases the exact match percentage in each comparison group, but the differences are not statistically significant according to a χ-square test.

4.3 Detailed Analyses

The effect of the dependency length feature on the distribution of dependency lengths is illustrated in Table 5. The table shows the mean of the total dependency length of each realized derivation compared to the corresponding gold standard derivation, as well as the number of derivations with greater and lower dependency length. According to paired t-tests, the mean dependency lengths for the DEPLEN-NODIST and DEPLEN models do not differ significantly from the gold standard. In contrast, the mean dependency length of all the models that do not in-

[3]Kudos to Kevin Gimpel for making his resampling scripts available from `http://www.ark.cs.cmu.edu/MT/paired_bootstrap_v13a.tar.gz`.

Model	% DL Lower	% DL Greater	DL Mean	Signif
GOLD	n.a.	n.a.	41.02	-
GLOBAL	17.23	21.59	42.40	***
DEPLEN-GLOBAL	24.37	12.81	40.29	***
DEPORD-NONF	15.76	19.34	42.34	***
DEPORD-NODIST	14.58	19.06	42.03	***
DEPLEN-NODIST	17.75	14.82	40.87	n.s.
DEPORD-NF	14.96	17.65	41.58	***
DEPLEN	16.28	14.78	40.97	n.s.

Table 5: Dependency Length Compared to Corpus—percentage of realizations with dependency length less than and greater than gold standard, along with mean dependency length, whose significance is tested against gold; 1671 development set (Section 00) complete realizations analyzed

Model	%Short Long	%Long Short	%Eq	%Sing Const
GOLD	25.25	4.87	4.08	65.79
GLOBAL	23.15	7.86	3.94	65.04
DEPLEN-GLOBAL	24.58	5.57	4.09	65.76
DEPORD-NONF	23.13	6.61	4.03	66.23
DEPORD-NODIST	23.38	6.52	3.94	66.15
DEPLEN-NODIST	24.03	5.38	4.01	66.58
DEPORD-NF	23.74	5.92	3.96	66.40
DEPLEN	24.36	5.36	4.07	66.21

Table 6: Distribution of various kinds of post-verbal constituents in the development set (Section 00); 4692 gold cases considered

clude the dependency length feature does differ significantly ($p < 0.001$) from the gold standard. Additionally, all these models have more realizations with dependency length greater than the gold standard, in comparison to the dependency length minimizing models; this shows the efficacy of the dependency length feature in approximating the gold standard. Interestingly, the DEPLEN-GLOBAL model significantly undershoots the gold standard on mean dependency length, and has the most skewed distribution of sentences with greater vs. lesser dependency length than the gold standard.

Apart from studying dependency length directly, we also looked at one of the attested effects of dependency length minimization, viz. the tendency to prefer short-long post-verbal constituents in production (Temperley, 2007). The relative lengths of adjacent post-verbal constituents were computed and

Model	% Light Heavy	% Heavy Light	Signif
GOLD	8.60	0.36	-
GLOBAL	7.73	2.02	***
DEPLEN-GLOBAL	8.35	0.75	**
DEPORD-NONF	7.98	1.15	***
DEPORD-NODIST	8.04	1.12	***
DEPLEN-NODIST	8.23	0.45	n.s.
DEPORD-NF	8.26	0.71	**
DEPLEN	8.36	0.51	n.s.

Table 7: Distribution of heavy unequal constituents (length difference > 5) in Section 00; 4692 gold cases considered and significance tested against the gold standard using a χ-square test

their distribution is shown in Table 6. While calculating length, punctuation marks were excluded. Four kinds of constituents were found in the post-verbal domain. For every verb, apart from single constituents and equal length constituents, short-long and long-short sequences were also observed. Table 6 demonstrates that for both the gold standard corpus as well as the realizer models, short-long constituents were more frequent than long-short or equal length constituents. This follows the trend reported by previous corpus studies of English (Temperley, 2007; Wasow and Arnold, 2003). The figures reported here show the tendency of the DEPLEN* models to be closer to the gold standard than the other models, especially in the case of short-long constituents.

We also performed an analysis of relative constituent lengths focusing on light-heavy and heavy-light cases; specifically, we examined unequal length constituent sequences where the length difference of the constituents was greater than 5, and the shorter constituent was under 5 words. Table 7 shows the results. Using a χ-square test, the distribution of heavy unequal length constituent counts in the DEPLEN-NODIST and DEPLEN models does not significantly differ from that of the gold standard. In contrast, for all the other models, the counts do differ significantly from the gold standard.

4.4 Interim Discussion

The experiments show a consistent positive effect of the dependency length feature in improving BLEU scores and achieving a better match with the corpus

Model	% Preferred	% Agr	Signif
GLOBAL	22	-	-
DEPLEN-GLOBAL	78	84	***
DEPORD-NODIST	24	-	-
DEPLEN-NODIST	76	92	***
DEPORD-NF	26	-	-
DEPLEN	74	96	***

Table 8: Targeted Human Evaluation—percentage of realizations preferred by two human judges in a 2AFC test among the 25 development set sentences with the greatest differences in dependency length, with a binomial test for significance

distributions of dependency length and short/long constituent orders. The results in Table 7 are particulary encouraging, as they show that minimizing dependency length reduces the number of realizations in which a heavy constituent precedes a light one down to essentially the level of the corpus, thereby eliminating many realizations that can be expected to have egregious errors like those shown in the introduction.

Intriguingly, there is some evidence that a negatively weighted total dependency length feature can go too far in minimizing dependency length, in the absence of other informative features to counterbalance it. In particular, the DEPLEN-GLOBAL model in Table 5 has significantly lower dependency length than the corpus, but in the richer models with discriminative synactic and dependency ordering features, there are no significant differences. It may still be though that additional features are necessary to counteract the tendency towards dependency length minimization, for example to ensure that initial constituents play their intended role in establishing and continuing topics in discourse, as also observed in the introduction.

4.5 Targeted Human Evaluation

To determine whether heavy-light ordering differences often represent ordering errors, including egregious ones such as those in Table 1, we conducted a targeted human evaluation on examples of this kind. Specifically, for each of the DEPLEN* models and their corresponding models without the dependency length feature, we chose the 25 sentences from the development section whose realizations exhibited the greatest difference in dependency length between sibling constituents appearing in opposite orders, and asked two judges (not the authors) to choose which of the two realizations best expressed the meaning of the reference sentence in a grammatical and fluent way, with the choice forced (2AFC). Table 8 shows the results. Agreement between the judges was high, with only one disagreement on the realizations from the DEPLEN and DEPORD-NF models (involving an acceptable paraphrase), and only four disagreements on the DEPLEN-GLOBAL and GLOBAL realizations. Pooling the judgments, the preference for the DEPLEN* models was well above the chance level of 50% according to a binomial test ($p < 0.001$ in each case). Inspecting the data ourselves, we found that many of the items did indeed involve egregious ordering errors that the DEPLEN* models managed to avoid.

5 Conclusions

In this paper, we investigated dependency length minimization in the context of realization ranking, focusing on its potential to eliminate egregious ordering errors as well as better match the distributional characteristics of sentence orderings in news text. When added to a state-of-the-art, comprehensive realization ranking model, we showed that including a dense, global feature for minimizing total dependency length yields statistically significant improvements in BLEU scores and significantly reduces the number of egregious heavy-light ordering errors. Going beyond the BLEU metric, we also conducted a targeted human evaluation to confirm the utility of the dependency length feature in models of varying richness. Interestingly, even with the richest model, in some cases we found that the dependency length feature still appears to go too far in minimizing dependency length, suggesting that further counter-balancing features—especially ones for the sentence-initial position (Filippova and Strube, 2009)—warrant investigation in future work.

Acknowledgments

This work was supported in part by NSF grants no. IIS-1143635 and IIS-0812297. We thank the anonymous reviewers for helpful comments and discussion.

References

Arto Anttila, Matthew Adams, and Mike Speriosu. 2010. The role of prosody in the English dative alternation. *Language and Cognitive Processes*.

Jennifer E. Arnold, Thomas Wasow, Anthony Losongco, and Ryan Ginstrom. 2000. Heaviness vs. newness: The effects of structural complexity and discourse status on constituent ordering. *Language*, 76:28–55.

Jason Baldridge and Geert-Jan Kruijff. 2002. Coupling CCG and Hybrid Logic Dependency Semantics. In *Proc. ACL-02*.

H Branigan, M Pickering, and M Tanaka. 2008. Contributions of animacy to grammatical function assignment and word order during production. *Lingua*, 118(2):172–189.

Joan Bresnan, Anna Cueni, Tatiana Nikitina, and R. Harald Baayen. 2007. Predicting the Dative Alternation. *Cognitive Foundations of Interpretation*, pages 69–94.

Aoife Cahill and Arndt Riester. 2009. Incorporating information status into generation ranking. In *Proceedings of*, ACL-IJCNLP '09, pages 817–825, Morristown, NJ, USA. Association for Computational Linguistics.

Aoife Cahill, Martin Forst, and Christian Rohrer. 2007. Designing features for parse disambiguation and realisation ranking. In Miriam Butt and Tracy Holloway King, editors, *Proceedings of the 12th International Lexical Functional Grammar Conference*, pages 128–147. CSLI Publications, Stanford.

Stephen Clark and James R. Curran. 2007. Wide-Coverage Efficient Statistical Parsing with CCG and Log-Linear Models. *Computational Linguistics*, 33(4):493–552.

Vera Demberg and Frank Keller. 2008. Data from eye-tracking corpora as evidence for theories of syntactic processing complexity. *Cognition*, 109(2):193–210.

Katja Filippova and Michael Strube. 2007. Generating constituent order in German clauses. In *ACL 2007, Proceedings of the 45th Annual Meeting of the Association for Computational Linguistics, June 23-30, 2007, Prague, Czech Republic*. The Association for Computer Linguistics.

Katja Filippova and Michael Strube. 2009. Tree linearization in English: Improving language model based approaches. In *Proceedings of Human Language Technologies: The 2009 Annual Conference of the North American Chapter of the Association for Computational Linguistics, Companion Volume: Short Papers*, pages 225–228, Boulder, Colorado, June. Association for Computational Linguistics.

Edward Gibson. 1998. Linguistic complexity: Locality of syntactic dependencies. *Cognition*, 68:1–76.

Edward Gibson. 2000. Dependency locality theory: A distance-based theory of linguistic complexity. In Alec Marantz, Yasushi Miyashita, and Wayne O'Neil, editors, *Image, Language, brain: Papers from the First Mind Articulation Project Symposium*. MIT Press, Cambridge, MA.

Daniel Gildea and David Temperley. 2007. Optimizing grammars for minimum dependency length. In *ACL*.

John A. Hawkins. 1994. *A Performance Theory of Order and Constituency*. Cambridge University Press, New York.

John A. Hawkins. 2000. The relative order of prepositional phrases in English: Going beyond manner-place-time. *Language Variation and Change*, 11(03):231–266.

John A. Hawkins. 2001. Why are categories adjacent? *Journal of Linguistics*, 37:1–34.

Julia Hockenmaier and Mark Steedman. 2007. CCGbank: A Corpus of CCG Derivations and Dependency Structures Extracted from the Penn Treebank. *Computational Linguistics*, 33(3):355–396.

Julia Hockenmaier. 2003. *Data and models for statistical parsing with Combinatory Categorial Grammar*. Ph.D. thesis, University of Edinburgh.

Gerard Kempen and Karin Harbusch. 2004. Generating natural word orders in a semi-free word order language: Treebank-based linearization preferences for German. In Alexander F. Gelbukh, editor, *CICLing*, volume 2945 of *Lecture Notes in Computer Science*, pages 350–354. Springer.

Philipp Koehn. 2004. Statistical significance tests for machine translation evaluation. In Dekang Lin and Dekai Wu, editors, *Proceedings of EMNLP 2004*, pages 388–395, Barcelona, Spain, July. Association for Computational Linguistics.

R. L. Lewis and S. Vasishth. 2005. An activation-based model of sentence processing as skilled memory retrieval. *Cognitive Science*, 29:1–45, May.

Richard L. Lewis, Shravan Vasishth, and Julie Van Dyke. 2006. Computational principles of working memory in sentence comprehension. *Trends in Cognitive Sciences*, 10(10):447–454.

Kishore Papineni, Salim Roukos, Todd Ward, and Wei-Jing Zhu. 2002. BLEU: a method for automatic evaluation of machine translation. In *Proc. ACL-02*.

Rajakrishnan Rajkumar and Michael White. 2010. Designing agreement features for realization ranking. In *Coling 2010: Posters*, pages 1032–1040, Beijing, China, August. Coling 2010 Organizing Committee.

Rajakrishnan Rajkumar, Michael White, and Dominic Espinosa. 2009. Exploiting named entity classes in CCG surface realization. In *Proceedings of Human Language Technologies: The 2009 Annual Conference of the North American Chapter of the Association for Computational Linguistics, Companion Volume: Short Papers*, pages 161–164, Boulder, Colorado, June. Association for Computational Linguistics.

Neal Snider and Annie Zaenen. 2006. Animacy and syntactic structure: Fronted NPs in English. In M. Butt, M. Dalrymple, and T.H. King, editors, *Intelligent Linguistic Architectures: Variations on Themes by Ronald M. Kaplan*. CSLI Publications, Stanford.

Mark Steedman. 2000. *The Syntactic Process*. MIT Press.

David Temperley. 2007. Minimization of dependency length in written English. *Cognition*, 105(2):300 – 333.

Harry Tily. 2010. *The Role of Processing Complexity in Word Order Variation and Change*. Ph.D. thesis, Stanford University.

Erik Velldal and Stefan Oepen. 2005. Maximum entropy models for realization ranking. In *Proc. MT-Summit X*.

Thomas Wasow and Jennifer Arnold. 2003. *Post-verbal Constituent Ordering in English*. Mouton.

Tom Wasow. 2002. *Postverbal Behavior*. CSLI Publications, Stanford.

Michael White and Rajakrishnan Rajkumar. 2009. Perceptron reranking for CCG realization. In *Proceedings of the 2009 Conference on Empirical Methods in Natural Language Processing*, pages 410–419, Singapore, August. Association for Computational Linguistics.

Michael White. 2006. Efficient Realization of Coordinate Structures in Combinatory Categorial Grammar. *Research on Language & Computation*, 4(1):39–75.

Hiroko Yamashita and Franklin Chang. 2001. "Long before short" preference in the production of a head-final language. *Cognition*, 81.

Fractal Unfolding: A Metamorphic Approach to Learning to Parse Recursive Structure*

Whitney Tabor
whitney.tabor@uconn.edu

Pyeong Whan Cho
pyeong.cho@uconn.edu

Emily Szkudlarek
emilyszkudlarek@gmail.com

Department of Psychology and Cognitive Science Program
University of Connecticut
406 Babbidge Road
Storrs, CT 06269-1020

Abstract

We describe a computational framework for language learning and parsing in which dynamical systems navigate on fractal sets. We explore the predictions of the framework in an artificial grammar task in which humans and recurrent neural networks are trained on a language with recursive structure. The results provide evidence for the claim of the dynamical systems models that grammatical systems continuously metamorphose during learning. The present perspective permits structural comparison between the recursive representations in symbolic and neural network models.

1 Introduction

Some loci in the phrase structure systems of natural languages appear to employ center embedding recursion (Chomsky, 1957), or at least an approximation of it (Christiansen and Chater, 1999). For example, one can embed a clause within a clause in English, using the object-extracted relative clause construction (e.g., *the dog that the goat chased barked.*). But such recursion does not appear in every phrase and may not appear in every language (Everett, 2005). Therefore, the system that learns natural languages must have a way of recognizing recursion when it occurs. We are interested in the problem, How does a language learner, seeing only a finite amount of data, decide on an unbounded recursive interpretation?

Here, we use the term "finite state" to refer to a system that can only be in a finite number of states. We use the term "recursion" to refer to situations in which multiple embeddings require the use of an unbounded symbol memory to keep track of unfinished dependencies.[1] We focus here on the case of center-embedding recursion, which can be generated by a context free grammar (one symbol on the left of each rule, finitely many symbols on the right) or a push-down automaton (stack memory + finite state controller) but not by a finite state device (Hopcroft and Ullman, 1979).

One natural approach to the recursion recognition problem, recently explored by Perfors et al. (2011), involves Bayesian grammar selection. Perfors et al.'s model considered a range of grammars, including both finite state and context free grammars. Their system, parameterized by data from English-speaking children in the Childes Database selected a context free grammar. Several features of this approach are notable: (i) There is a rich set of structural assumptions (the grammars in the pool of candidates). (ii) Because many plausible grammars generate overlapping data sets, a complexity ranking is also assumed and the system operates under Occam's Razor: prefer simpler grammars. (iii) Grammar selection and on-line parsing are treated as sep-

*This material is based on work supported by the National Science Foundation Grant No. 1059662. We thank the members of SOLAB who helped run the experiment: Olivia Harold, Milod Kazerounian, Emily Pakstis, Bo Powers, Kevin Semataska.

[1]This is a narrow construal of the term "recursion". Sometimes the term is used for any situation in which a rule can be applied arbitrarily many times in the generation of a single sentence, including finite-state cases.

arate problems in that the system is evaluated for coverage of the observed sentences, but the particular method of parsing plays no role in the selection process.

Here, we focus on a contrasting approach: recurrent neural network models discover the structure of grammatical systems by sequentially processing the corpus data, attempting to predict after each word, what word will come next (Elman, 1990; Elman, 1991). With respect to the properties mentioned above, the neural network approach has some advantages: (i) Formal analyses of some of the networks and related systems (Moore, 1998; Siegelmann, 1999; Tabor, 2009b) indicate that these models make even richer structural assumptions than the Bayesian approach: if the networks have infinite precision, then some of them recognize all string languages, including non-computable ones. For a long while, theorists of cognition have adopted the view that positing a restrictive hypothesis space is desirable—otherwise a theory of structure would seem to have little substance. However, if one offers a hypothesis about the organization of the hypothesis space, and a principle that specifies the way a learning organism navigates in the space, then the theory can still make strong, testable predictions. We suggest that assuming a very general function class is preferable to presupposing arbitrary grammar or class restrictions. (ii) The recurrent networks do not employ an independently defined complexity metric. Instead, the learning process successively breaks symmetries in the initially unbiased weight set, driven by asymmetries in the data. The result is a bias toward simplicity. We see this as an advantage in that the simplicity preference stems from the form of the architecture and learning mechanism. (iii) Word-by-word parsing and grammar selection occur as part of a single process—the network updates its weights every time it processes a word and this results in the formation of a parsing system. We see this as an advantage in that the moment-to-moment interaction of the system with data resembles the circumstances of a learning child.

On the other hand, there has long been a serious difficulty with the network approach: the network dynamics and solutions have been very opaque to analysis. Although the systems sometimes learn well and capture data effectively, they are not scientifically very revealing unless we can interpret them. The Bayesian grammar-selection approach is much stronger in this regard: the formal properties of the grammars employed are well understood and the selection process is well-grounded in statistical theory—e.g., Griffiths et al. (2010).

Here, we take advantage of recent formal results indicating how recurrent neural networks can encode abstract recursive structure (Moore, 1998; Pollack, 1987; Siegelmann, 1999; Tabor, 2000) An essential insight is that the network can use a spatial recursive structure, a fractal, to encode the temporal recursive structure of a symbol sequence. When the network is trained on short sentences exhibiting a few levels of embedding, it tends to generalize to higher levels of embedding, suggesting that it is not merely shaping itself to the training data, but discovers an abstract principle (Rodriguez et al., 1999; Rodriguez, 2001; Tabor, 2003; Wiles and Elman, 1995). During the course of learning, the fractal comes into being gradually in such a way that lower-order finite-state approximations to the recursion develop before higher-order structure does—a complexity cline phenomenon (Tabor, 2003).

We examined human and neural network learning of a recursive language with an artificial grammar paradigm, the Box Prediction paradigm. Whereas our previous investigations of this task (Cho et al., 2011) focused on counting recursion languages (only a single stack symbol is required to track the recursive dependencies), we provide evidence here for mirror recursion learning by a few participants (multiple stack symbols required). We show how the theory of fractal grammars can be used to hand wire a network that processes the recursive language of our task. We then provide evidence that a Simple Recurrent Network (Elman, 1990; Elman, 1991), trained on the same task, also develops a fractal encoding. Moreover, the network shows evidence of a embodying a complexity-cline—similarly complex grammars are adjacent in the parameter space. An individual differences analysis indicates that a similar pattern arises in the humans. We conclude that the network encodings can be formally related to symbolic recursive models, but are different in that learning occurs by continuous grammar metamorphosis.

2 The Box Prediction paradigm

Human participants sat in front of a computer screen on which five black outlines of boxes were displayed (Figure 1). When the participant clicked on the screen, one of the boxes changed color. The task was to indicate, by clicking on it, which box would change color next on each trial. The sequence of color changes corresponded to the structure of sentences generated by the center-embedding grammar in Table 1a. The sentences can be divided into embedding level classes. Level n sentences have (n-1) center-embedded clauses (Table 1b). There were three, distinct phases of the color-change sequence: during the first 60 trials, participants saw only Level 1 sentences. From trials 61 to 410, Level 2 sentences were introduced with increasing frequency. We refer to these two phases of presentation together as the "Training Phase". Starting at Trial 411, Level 3 sentences were included, along with more Level 1 and Level 2 sentences. We refer to the trials from 411 to 553, the end of the experiment, as the "Test Phase". Other than by their structural differences, these phases were not distinguished for the participants: the participants experienced them as one, long sequence of 553 trials. We introduced the deeper levels of embedding gradually because of evidence from the language acquisition literature (Newport, 1990), from the connectionist literature (Elman, 1993), and from the artificial grammar learning literature (Cho et al., 2011; Lai and Poletiek, 2011) that "starting small" facilitates learning of complex syntactic structures. Following standard terminology, we call the trials in which boxes 1 and 4 change colors "push" trials (because in a natural implementation of the grammar with a pushdown automaton, the automaton pushes a symbol onto the stack at these trials). We call the trials in which boxes 2, 3, and 5 change color "pop" trials. The push trials were fairly unpredictable: the choice of whether to push 1 or 4 was approximately uniformly distributed throughout the experiment, and the choice about whether to embed was fairly random within the constraints of the "starting small" scheme described above. Because we did not want participants to have to guess at these nondeterministic events, we made the 1 and 4 boxes turn blue or green whenever they occurred and told the participants that they did not need to predict blue or green boxes. On the other hand, we wanted them to predict the pop trials whenever they occurred. Therefore, we colored boxes 2, 3, and 5 a shade of red whenever they occurred and told the participants that they should try to predict all boxes that turned a shade of red. When two of the same symbol occurred in a row (e.g., 1 1 2 2 5), we shifted the shade of the color of the repeated element so that participants would notice the change. To reinforce this visual feedback, a beep sounded on any trial in which a participant failed to predict a box that changed to a shade of red. Box 5 has a different structural status than the other boxes: it marks the ends of sentences. We included box 5, placing it in the center of the visual array, and making it smaller than the other boxes, to make the task easier relative to a pilot version in which Box 5 was absent.

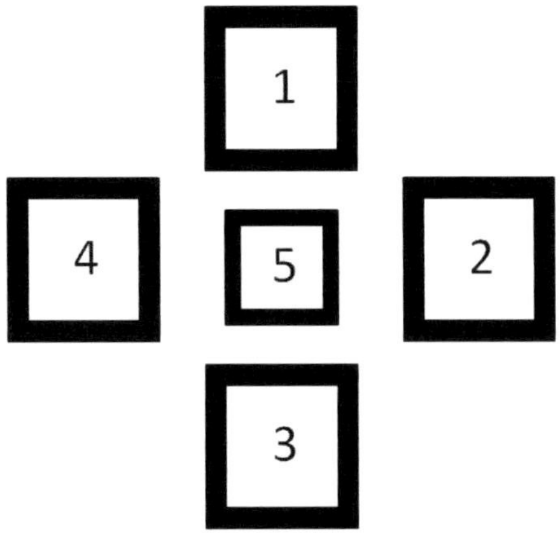

Figure 1: Structure of the display for the Box Prediction Task. The numerals were not present in the screen display shown to the participants.

2.1 Simulation Experiment

We employed Michal Cernansky's implementation of Elman (1990)'s Simple Recurrent Network (http://www2.fiit.stuba.sk/černans/main/download.html). The network had five input units, five output units and ten hidden units. Activations changed as specified in (1) and weights changed according to (2).

a.	Root	→	S 5	
	S	→	1 S 2	
	S	→	1 2	
	S	→	4 S 3	
	S	→	4 3	
b.	Level 1	Level 2	Level 3	
	1 2 5	1 1 2 2 5	1 1 1 2 2 2 5	
	4 3 5	1 4 3 2 5	1 1 4 3 2 2 5	
		4 1 2 3 5	1 4 1 2 3 2 5	
		4 4 3 3 5	2 4 4 3 3 2 5	
			...	

Table 1: a. Grammar 1: a recursive grammar for generating the color change sequence employed in the experiment. "Root" is the initial node of every sentence generation process. *Null* stands for the empty string. b. Examples of Level 1, 2, and 3 sentences generated by Grammar 1.

$$\begin{aligned} \vec{h}(t) &= f(\mathbf{Whh} \cdot \vec{h}(t-1) + \mathbf{Whi} \cdot \vec{s}(t) + \vec{b}_h) \\ \vec{o}(t) &= f(\mathbf{Woh} \cdot \vec{h}(t) + \vec{b}_o) \\ f(x) &= \frac{1}{1+e^{-x}} \end{aligned} \tag{1}$$

$$\Delta w_{ij} \propto -\frac{\partial E}{\partial w_{ij}} \tag{2}$$

Here, $\vec{s}(t)$ is the vector of input unit activations at time step t, $\mathbf{Whi}$ are the weights from input to hidden units, $\mathbf{Whh}$ are the recurrent hidden connections, and $\mathbf{Woh}$ connect hidden to output.

On each trial, the input to the network was an indexical bit vector corresponding to one of the five sentence symbols. The task of the network was to predict, on its output layer, what symbol would occur next at each point. The sequence of symbols was modeled on the sequence presented to the human participants as follows: the human sequence was divided into 14 nearly equal-length segments, each with a whole number of sentences (the first 11 segments corresponded to the Training Phase and the last 3 to the Test Phase). Each segment contained approximately ten sentences. For each segment, 400 sentences were sampled randomly according to the distribution of types found in the segment. These groups of 400 were concatenated end to end to form the training sequence for the network (a total of 22398 trials).

The error gradient of equation (2) was approximated using Backpropagation Through Time (Rumelhart et al., 1986) with eight time steps unfolded. To simulate the absence of negative feedback on push trials in the human experiment, the network error signal on push trials was set to zero. The constant of proportionality in equation 2 (the "learning rate") was set to 0.4.

3 Fractal Encoding of Recursive Structure in Neural Ensembles

In the past several decades, a number of researchers (Moore, 1998; Pollack, 1987; Siegelmann, 1996; Siegelmann and Sontag, 1994; Tabor, 2000) have developed devices for symbol processing which compute on finite-dimensional complete metric spaces (distance is defined, no points are "missing"— (Bryant, 1985)), like the neural networks considered here. A common strategy in all of these proposals is the use of spatially recursive sets—i.e., fractals—to encode the temporal recursive structure in symbol sequences. For example, Tabor (2000) defines a *Dynamical Automaton* (or DA), M, as in (3).

$$M = (H, F, P, \Sigma, IM, x_0, FR) \tag{3}$$

Here, H is a complete metric space (Bryant, 1985; Barnsley, 1993). F is a finite list of functions $f_i : H \to H$, P is a partition of the metric space, Σ is a finite symbol alphabet, IM is an *Input Map*—that is, a function from symbols in Σ and compartments in P to functions in F. The input to the machine is a finite string of symbols. The machine starts at x_0 and invokes functions corresponding the symbols in the input in the order in which they occur. If, when the last symbol has been presented, the system is in the region $FR \subseteq H$, then the DA *accepts* the string.

Table 3 specifies DA 1, a dynamical automaton that recognizes (and generates) the language of Grammar 1. A good way of understanding the principle underlying this mechanism is to note that a pushdown automaton (PDA) (Hopcroft and Ullman, 1979) for processing this language must employ a stack alphabet with one symbol for tracking"1" and another for tracking "4". (See Table 3). If DA 1 is to successfully process the same language, it must distinguish at least the states that PDA 1 distinguishes

(PDA 1 is minimal in this sense). DA 1 does this by executing state transitions analogous to the push and pop operations of the PDA, arriving in its final region when the PDA is in an accepting state. Figure 3 shows the correspondence between machine states of PDA 1 and points in the metric space H that underlies DA 1's language recognition capability. This figure makes it clear that DA 1 is structurally equivalent to PDA 1.

The computing framework discussed here is very general. One can construct a fractal grammar that generates any context free language (Tabor, 2000). In fact, similar mechanisms recognize and generate not only all computable languages but all languages of strings drawn from a finite alphabet (Moore, 1998; Siegelmann, 1999; Siegelmann and Sontag, 1994). Wiles & Elman (1995) and Rodriguez (2001) showed that an SRN trained on a counting recursion language ($a^n b^n$) uses a fractal principle to keep track of the embeddings and generalizes to deeper levels of embedding than those found in its training set. (Tabor et al., 2003) showed that a gradient descent mechanism operating in the parameter space of a fractal grammar model discovered close approximations of several mirror recursion languages. These findings suggest that the fractal solutions are stable equilibria ("attractors") of recurrent network gradient descent learning processes (Tabor, 2011). This observation argues against a widespread belief about neural networks that they are blank slate architectures, only performing "associative processing" without structural generalization (Fodor and Pylyshyn, 1988). It suggests a close relationship between the classical theory of computation and neural network models even though the two frameworks are not equivalent (Siegelmann, 1999; Tabor, 2009a) .

The results of Tabor (2003) indicate that network learning proceeds along a complexity cline: sentences with lower levels of embedding are correctly processed before sentences with higher levels of embedding. This indicates that there are proximity relationships in the network parameter space: parameterizations that parse successively deeper levels of embedding are adjacent to each other. In the next section, we investigate the outcome of the SRN learning experiment with the Box Prediction training data, first testing for evidence that the network forms a fractal code, then testing for a proximity effect consistent with the complexity cline prediction.

$M = (Q, \Sigma, \Gamma, \delta, q_0, Z_0, F)$
$Q = \{q_1, q_2, q_3\}$
$\Sigma = \{1, 2, 3, 4, 5\}, \Gamma = \{B, O, F\}$
$q_0 = q_3, Z_0 = B, F = B$

$\delta(q3, 1, B) = (q1, OB), \delta(q3, 4, B) = (q1, FB)$
$\delta(q1, 1, O) = (q1, OO), \delta(q1, 4, O) = (q1, FO)$
$\delta(q1, 1, F) = (q1, OF), \delta(q1, 4, F) = (q1, FF)$
$\delta(q1, 2, O) = (q2, \epsilon), \delta(q2, 2, O) = (q2, \epsilon)$
$\delta(q1, 3, F) = (q2, \epsilon), \delta(q2, 3, F) = (q2, \epsilon)$
$\delta(q2, 5, B) = (q3, B)$

Table 3: PDA 1. A Pushdown Automaton for processing the language of Grammar 1. "O" is pushed on "1". "F" is pushed on "4".

4 Results: Simple Recurrent Network Box Prediction

We trained 71 networks, corresponding to the 71 human participants on the sequence described above in Section 2. The networks all used the same architecture, but differed in the values of their random initial weights and the precise ordering of the training sentences (although all used the same progressive scheme described above). To approximate the observed variation in human performance, each network also had gaussian noise with constant variance added to the weights with each new word input. The variance values were sampled from the uniform distribution on [0,4]. This range was chosen to produce a mean (57%) and standard deviation (20%) similar to that of the humans at the end of training ($M = 51\%, SD = 21\%$).

Unlike some of the humans, none of the networks generalized immediately to Level 3 sentences on the first try. Nevertheless, several of them learned to parse the Level 3 sentences with very few errors by the end of the "Test Phase". To determine accuracy of a deterministic transition, we normalized the network output vector by dividing all the outputs by the sum of the outputs. If the highest normalized activation was on the correct transition, we counted the transition as accurate. When tested on all eight types of Level 3 sentences, the top 4 networks made 1, 3, 3, and 3 errors among the 56 transitions in this sen-

Compartment	Symbol	Function
$h_1 > 0 \,\&\, h_2 > 0$	1	$\vec{h} \leftarrow \begin{bmatrix} \frac{1}{2} & 0 \\ 0 & \frac{1}{2} \end{bmatrix} \vec{h} + \begin{pmatrix} 1 \\ 0 \end{pmatrix}$
$h_1 > 0 \,\&\, h_2 > 0$	4	$\vec{h} \leftarrow \begin{bmatrix} \frac{1}{2} & 0 \\ 0 & \frac{1}{2} \end{bmatrix} \vec{h} + \begin{pmatrix} 0 \\ 0 \end{pmatrix}$
$h_1 > 1$	2	$\vec{h} \leftarrow \begin{bmatrix} -2 & 0 \\ 0 & -2 \end{bmatrix} \vec{h} + \begin{pmatrix} 2 \\ 0 \end{pmatrix}$
$0 < h_1 < 1$	3	$\vec{h} \leftarrow \begin{bmatrix} -2 & 0 \\ 0 & -2 \end{bmatrix} \vec{h} + \begin{pmatrix} 0 \\ 0 \end{pmatrix}$
$h_1 < -1$	2	$\vec{h} \leftarrow \begin{bmatrix} 2 & 0 \\ 0 & 2 \end{bmatrix} \vec{h} + \begin{pmatrix} 2 \\ 0 \end{pmatrix}$
$-1 < h_1 \,\&\, h_1 < 1$	3	$\vec{h} \leftarrow \begin{bmatrix} 2 & 0 \\ 0 & 2 \end{bmatrix} \vec{h} + \begin{pmatrix} 0 \\ 0 \end{pmatrix}$
$h_1 = -1 \,\&\, h_2 = -1$	5	$\vec{h} \leftarrow \begin{bmatrix} -1 & 0 \\ 0 & -1 \end{bmatrix} \vec{h} + \begin{pmatrix} 0 \\ 0 \end{pmatrix}$

Table 2: Input Map for DA 1. The automaton starts at the point, (1, 1). It's Final Region is also (1, 1).

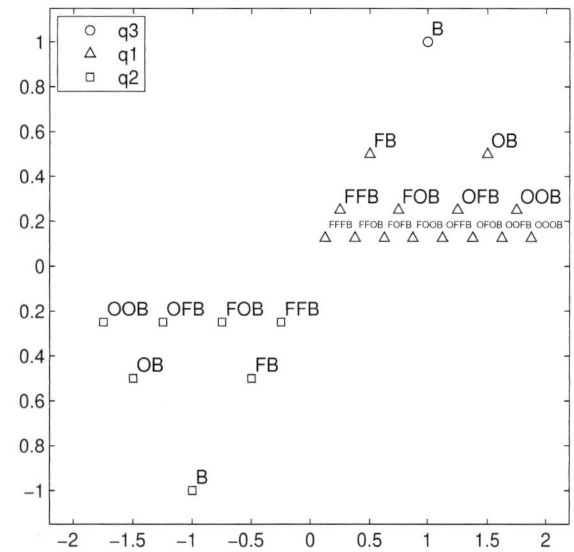

Figure 2: Correspondence between states of DA 1 and PDA stack states.

tence set.

We hypothesized that the networks were approximating a fractal grammar with the same qualitative structure as that of DA 1, possibly in more than two dimensions. We sought two kinds of evidence: "linear separability" and "branching structure". For "linear separability", we asked if the SRN states corresponding to a particular point in DA 1 (state of PDA 1) were clustered so as to be linearly separable from SRN states corresponding to a different point. Two sets A and B of points in a vector space of dimension n are *linearly separable* if there is an $n - 1$ dimensional hyperplane in the space with all the points of A on one side of it and all the points of B on the other. In fractal grammar parsing, pairwise linear separability suffices to distinguish the machine states (Tabor, 2000). Among the cases where more than one sample point corresponded to the same PDA state, an average of 17.6/22 were pairwise linearly separable from the other groups. In six of the networks, all the multi-element clusters were pairwise linearly separable. This finding lends support to the claim that the networks approximate fractal grammars.

For "branching structure", we asked if the deployment of these (largely) linearly separable clusters corresponded to the branching structure of the fractal of DA 1. In particular, for each cluster corresponding to a DA 1/PDA 1 state with more than one symbol on the stack in PDA 1, we considered all the clusters with one-fewer symbols on the stack. We asked if the nearest cluster with one fewer symbols on the stack corresponded to the nearest one-fewer stack symbol point in DA 1. In Level 1 to and 3 sentences, there are 20 such states to consider. Across networks, the average rate of unexpected proximity relationships was 3.5/20 (SD = 1.7). The best networks we observed under this training method (noise reduced to 0) generated only 1 unexpected proximity relationship. These results also indicate a close correspondence between the organization of the network and fractal grammars.

Up to this point, the evidence we have been presenting has supported a formal correspondence between SRNs and fractal grammars. In the final part of this section, we consider one prediction of the network approach that is not obviously predicted by symbolic grammar mixture accounts like the Bayesian model discussed in the introduction.

Tabor (2003) shows how a fractal for processing another recursive language (similar to the language of Grammar 1) arises by gradual metamorphosis of (Stage I) a single point into (Stage II) a line of points, then into (Stage III) an infinite lattice, then into (Stage IV) a fractal with overlapping branches and finally into (Stage V) the fully-formed fractal that very closely captures the recursive embedding structure. During Stage IV, the system correctly processes shallow levels of embedding but fails to process deeper levels of embedding. As the metamorphosis progresses, this Fractal Learning Neural Network (FLNN) becomes able to process deeper and deeper levels at an accelerating rate such that, after finite time, it reaches a point where it is effectively processing all levels, indicating a continuous complexity cline in parameter space. An empirical implication is that a network that has mastered n levels of embedding, for n a natural number, will more easily (with less weight change) master n+1 levels of embedding than one that has mastered fewer than n.

To see if the SRN's complexity cline predictions are in line with those of the FLNNs, we correlated the network's performance at the end of the Training Phase with its performance in the Test Phase. For this purpose, we defined the training performance as the mean prediction accuracy across all predictable transitions of Level 1 and 2 sentences in the fourth quarter of the training phase. The Test Phase performance was defined in two different ways. It was defined as the mean accuracy across novel but predictable transitions (a) in all Level 3 sentences in the test phase or (b) only in the first instances of four different Level 3 sentences. We used the second measure because the networks and humans continue to learn in the Test Phase: correlation of training performance with measure (a) might stem from learning facility alone; correlation with (b) indicates generalization ability. Both tests showed significant correlation (a: $r(69) = 0.98, p < .0001$; b: $r(69) = 53, p < .0001$). These results are consistent with the claim that the SRN induces a complexity cline similar to that induced by the fractal learning networks..

To consider how well this prediction distinguishes the fractal learning framework from other approaches to grammar learning, we now consider the Bayesian grammar selection model of (Perfors et al., 2011). We consider this case, which is naturally related to our focus, as a first step toward developing concrete approaches within the Bayesian framework that could address the issues raised by the Box Prediction findings.

Perfors et al.'s model is also concerned with the induction of recursive grammatical systems from language data. They presented samples from the Childes Database (MacWhinney, 2000) to their model over 6 stages, where each stage sampled the corpus more thoroughly than the last. This sampling method generally caused each stage to have heavier sampling of deeper recursive structures than the previous stage because the deeper recursive structures are less frequent in the master corpus. The Bayesian model selects finite-state grammars during the earlier stages and then prefers recursive grammars during the later stages. This shift occurs because, as the sampling goes deeper, the finite state systems need to employ many additional productions to handle the burgeoning variety of collocations, while the recursive grammars can handle them with few rules, so the model's anti-complexity bias causes it to prefer the recursive grammars (Perfors et al., p. 320). It seems likely that a version of their model, applied to the training data in our experiment, would select finite-state grammars during the Training Phase and the switch to a recursive grammar in the Test Phase. Perfors et al. did not consider the question of individual differences. We can think of one way that the basic correlational finding reported for the SRNs would obtain in the Bayesian system (finding (a) above): if the perception of the stimuli by some models was noisier than that of others, then one expects the general correlation between Training and Test performance to obtain: the noise interferes similarly with both phases so correlated accuracy is observed. It is not as clear to us that the Bayesian system will predict finding (b), which shows that first-try performance on novel structures is better for people who show better Training performance.[2] There does not appear to be a proximity relationship between grammars in Perfors et al.'s model as there is in the network models. Thus, if it predicts this effect, then it would have to do so for a different reason, a point worthy of further research.

5 Results: Human Box Prediction

Seventy-one undergraduate students in the University of Connecticut participated in the experiment for course credit. The range of human performance was substantial. The mean correct performance on 37 predictable trials during the last 100 trials of training was 51% (SD = 21%). Despite this overall low rate of performance at test, there was a subset of people who learned the training grammar well by the end of training.

Twelve of the 71 participants, scored over 80% correct on the pop trials within the last 100 training trials. 80% is the level of correct performance that a particular finite-state device we refer to as the "Simple Markov Model" would yield during these 100 trials. The Simple Markov Model predicts 2 after 1, 3 after 2, 4 after 3, and 1 after 4. The two top scorers among these twelve generalized perfectly to each first instance of the four Level 3 types in the test phase. If, contrary to our hypothesis, all 12 were using finite state mechanisms, and they guessed randomly on novel transitions, the chances of observing 2 or more perfect scorers would be 0.9% (p = .009). We take this as evidence that the two strongest generalizers developed a representation closely approximating a recursive system.

Performance at the end of training correlated with accuracy on 24 novel transitions in Level 3 sentences at test ($r(69) = 0.72, p < .0001$). This corresponds to test (a) of the SRN Results section above, suggesting some kind of grammar proximity model. Regarding (b), accuracy on the 8 novel transitions in the 4 first instances of novel Level 3 sentences also correlated with the performance at the end of training, $r(69) = 0.57, p < .0001$. These results lend some empirical support to the complexity cline predictions of the fractal model.

[2]This is not single-trial learning. It is immediate generalization to unseen cases.

6 General Discussion

We studied the learning of recursion by training Simple Recurrent Networks (SRNs) and humans in an artificial grammar task. We described metric space computing models that navigate on fractal sets and noted a complexity cline phenomenon in learning (learning of lower embeddings facilitates the learning of higher ones). Previous work in this area has focused on counting recursion languages. Here, we explored learning of a mirror recursion language. We showed that the SRN hidden unit representations had clustering and branching structure approximating the predictions of the fractal grammar model. They also showed evidence of the complexity cline. The human learning results on the same language provided evidence that at least a few people inferred a recursive principle for the mirror recursion language. The complexity cline prediction was also borne out by the human data: not only did performance on lower levels of embedding correlate with performance on higher levels of embedding, but it predicted generalization behavior, suggesting that the representation continuously metamorphoses from a finite-state system into an infinite state system.

We identified one closely related Bayesian grammar induction model (Perfors et al., 2011) which seems well positioned to make similar, but probably not the same, predictions about phenomenon of infinite state language learning. We suggest that further exploration of the relationship between the Bayesian models and the recurrent neural network models will be helpful. A novel claim of the present work is that they it is possible to compare recurrent neural network models and symbolic structure models on the same terms. We suggest that further examination of this relationship may be helpful in addressing the challenging problems of complex language learning.

References

Michael Barnsley. 1993. *Fractals Everywhere, 2nd ed.* Academic Press, Boston.

Victor Bryant. 1985. *Metric Spaces. Iteration and Application.* Cambridge University Press, Cambridge, UK.

Pyeong Whan Cho, Emily Szkudlarek, Anuenue Kukona, and Whitney Tabor. 2011. An artificial grammar investigation into the mental encoding of syntactic structure. In Laura Carlson, Christoph Hoelscher, and Thomas F. Shipley, editors, *Proceedings of the 33rd Annual Meeting of the Cognitive Science Society (Cogsci2011)*, pages 1679–1684, Austin, TX. Cognitive Science Society. Available online at http://palm.mindmodeling.org/cogsci2011/.

Noam Chomsky. 1957. *Syntactic Structures.* Mouton and Co., The Hague.

Morten H. Christiansen and Nick Chater. 1999. Toward a connectionist model of recursion in human linguistic performance. *Cognitive Science*, 23:157–205.

Jeffrey L. Elman. 1990. Finding structure in time. *Cognitive Science*, 14:179–211.

Jeffrey L. Elman. 1991. Distributed representations, simple recurrent networks, and grammatical structure. *Machine Learning*, 7:195–225.

Jeffrey L. Elman. 1993. Learning and development in neural networks: the importance of starting small. *Cognition*, 48:71–99.

Daniel L. Everett. 2005. Cultural constraints on grammar and cognition in Piraha: another look at the design features of human language. *Current Anthropology*, 46(4):621–646, August.

J. A. Fodor and Z. W. Pylyshyn. 1988. Connectionistm and cognitive architecture: A critical analysis. *Cognition*, 28:3–71.

Thomas L. Griffiths, Nick Chater, Charles Kemp, Amy Perfors, and Joshua B. Tenenbaum. 2010. Probabilistic models of cognition: exploring representations and inductive biases. *Trends in Cognitive Sciences*, 14(8):357–364.

John E. Hopcroft and Jeffrey D. Ullman. 1979. *Introduction to Automata Theory, Languages, and Computation.* Addison-Wesley, Menlo Park, California.

Jun Lai and Fenna H. Poletiek. 2011. The impact of adjacent-dependencies and staged-input on the learnability of center-embedded hierarchical structures. *Cognition*, 118(2):265–273, February.

B. MacWhinney. 2000. *The CHILDES project: Tools for analyzing talk.* Lawrence Erlbaum Associates, Mahwah, NJ, third edition.

Cris Moore. 1998. Dynamical recognizers: Real-time language recognition by analog computers. *Theoretical Computer Science*, 201:99–136.

Elissa L. Newport. 1990. Maturational constraints on language learning. *Cognitive Science*, 14(1):11–28, March.

Amy Perfors, Joshua B. Tenenbaum, and Terry Regier. 2011. The learnability of abstract syntactic principles. *Cognition*, 118(3):306–338, December.

Jordan Pollack. 1987. On connectionist models of natural language processing. Unpublished doctoral dissertation, University of Illinois.

Paul Rodriguez, Janet Wiles, and Jeffrey Elman. 1999. A recurrent neural network that learns to count. *Connection Science*, 11(1):5–40.

Paul Rodriguez. 2001. Simple recurrent networks learn context-free and context-sensitive languages by counting. *Neural Computation*, 13(9):2093–2118.

David E. Rumelhart, Geoffrey E. Hinton, and R. J. Williams. 1986. Learning internal representations by error propagation. In David E. Rumelhart, James L. McClelland, and the PDP Research Group, editors, *Parallel Distributed Processing, v. 1*, pages 318–362. MIT Press.

H. T. Siegelmann and E. D. Sontag. 1994. Analog computation via neural networks. *Theoretical Computer Science*, 131:331–360.

Hava Siegelmann. 1996. The simple dynamics of super Turing theories. *Theoretical Computer Science*, 168:461–472.

Hava T. Siegelmann. 1999. *Neural Networks and Analog Computation: Beyond the Turing Limit.* Birkhäuser, Boston.

Whitney Tabor, Bruno Galantucci, and Daniel Richardson. 2003. Evidence for self-organized sentence processing: Local coherence effects. Submitted manuscript, University of Connecticut, Department of Psychology: See http://www.sp.uconn.edu/ ps300vc/papers.html.

Whitney Tabor. 2000. Fractal encoding of context-free grammars in connectionist networks. *Expert Systems: The International Journal of Knowledge Engineering and Neural Networks*, 17(1):41–56.

Whitney Tabor. 2003. Learning exponential state growth languages by hill climbing. *IEEE Transactions on Neural Networks*, 14(2):444–446.

Whitney Tabor. 2009a. Affine dynamical automata. Ms., University of Connecticut Department of Psychology.

Whitney Tabor. 2009b. A dynamical systems perspective on the relationship between symbolic and non-symbolic computation. *Cognitive Neurodynamics*, 3(4):415–427.

Whitney Tabor. 2011. Recursion and recursion-like structure in ensembles of neural elements. In H. Sayama, A. Minai, D. Braha, and Y. Bar-Yam, editors, *Unifying Themes in Complex Sys-*

tems. Proceedings of the VIII International Conference on Complex Systems, pages 1494–1508, Cambridge, MA. New England Complex Systems Institute. http//necsi.edu/events/iccs2011/proceedings.html.

Janet Wiles and Jeff Elman. 1995. Landscapes in recurrent networks. In Johanna D. Moore and Jill Fain Lehman, editors, *Proceedings of the 17th Annual Cognitive Science Conference*. Lawrence Erlbaum Associates.

Connectionist-Inspired Incremental PCFG Parsing

Marten van Schijndel
The Ohio State University
vanschm@ling.ohio-state.edu

Andy Exley
University of Minnesota
exley@cs.umn.edu

William Schuler
The Ohio State University
schuler@ling.ohio-state.edu

Abstract

Probabilistic context-free grammars (PCFGs) are a popular cognitive model of syntax (Jurafsky, 1996). These can be formulated to be sensitive to human working memory constraints by application of a right-corner transform (Schuler, 2009). One side-effect of the transform is that it guarantees at most a single expansion (push) and at most a single reduction (pop) during a syntactic parse. The primary finding of this paper is that this property of right-corner parsing can be exploited to obtain a dramatic reduction in the number of random variables in a probabilistic sequence model parser. This yields a simpler structure that more closely resembles existing simple recurrent network models of sentence comprehension.

1 Introduction

There may be a benefit to using insights from human cognitive modelling in parsing. Evidence for incremental processing can be seen in garden pathing (Bever, 1970), close shadowing (Marslen-Wilson, 1975), and eyetracking studies (Tanenhaus et al., 1995; Allopenna et al., 1998; Altmann and Kamide, 1999), which show humans begin attempting to process a sentence immediately upon receiving linguistic input. In the cognitive science community, this incremental interaction has often been modelled using recurrent neural networks (Elman, 1991; Mayberry and Miikkulainen, 2003), which utilize a hidden context with a severely bounded representational capacity (a fixed number of continuous units or dimensions), similar to models of activation-based memory in the prefrontal cortex (Botvinick, 2007), with the interesting possibility that the distributed behavior of neural columns (Horton and Adams, 2005) may directly implement continuous dimensions of recurrent hidden units. This paper presents a refinement of a factored probabilistic sequence model of comprehension (Schuler, 2009) in the direction of a recurrent neural network model and presents some observed efficiencies due to this refinement.

This paper will adopt an incremental probabilistic context-free grammar (PCFG) parser (Schuler, 2009) that uses a right-corner variant of the left-corner parsing strategy (Aho and Ullman, 1972) coupled with strict memory bounds, as a model of human-like parsing. Syntax can readily be approximated using simple PCFGs (Hale, 2001; Levy, 2008; Demberg and Keller, 2008), which can be easily tuned (Petrov and Klein, 2007). This paper will show that this representation can be streamlined to exploit the fact that a right-corner parse guarantees at most one expansion and at most one reduction can take place after each word is seen (see Section 2.2). The primary finding of this paper is that this property of right-corner parsing can be exploited to obtain a dramatic reduction in the number of random variables in a probabilistic sequence model parser (Schuler, 2009) yielding a simpler structure that more closely resembles connectionist models such as TRACE (McClelland and Elman, 1986), Shortlist (Norris, 1994; Norris and McQueen, 2008), or recurrent models (Elman, 1991; Mayberry and Miikkulainen, 2003) which posit functional units only for cognitively-motivated entities.

The rest of this paper is structured as follows: Section 2 gives the formal background of the right-corner parser transform and probabilistic sequence model parsing. The simplification of this model is described in Section 3. A discussion of the interplay between cognitive theory and computational modelling in the resulting model may be found in Section 4. Finally, Section 5 demonstrates that such factoring also yields large benefits in the speed of probabilistic sequence model parsing.

2 Background

2.1 Notation

Throughout this paper, PCFG rules are defined over syntactic categories subscripted with abstract tree addresses ($c_{\eta\iota}$). These addresses describe a node's location as a path from a given ancestor node. A 0 on this path represents a leftward branch and a 1 a rightward branch. Positions within a tree are represented by subscripted η and ι so that $c_{\eta 0}$ is the left child of c_η and $c_{\eta 1}$ is the right child of c_η. The set of syntactic categories in the grammar is denoted by C. Finally, $[\![\phi]\!]$ denotes an *indicator* probability which is 1 if ϕ and 0 otherwise.

2.2 Right-Corner Parsing

Parsers such as that of Schuler (2009) model hierarchically deferred processes in working memory using a coarse analogy to a pushdown store indexed by an embedding depth d (to a maximum depth D). To make efficient use of this store, a CFG G must be transformed using a right-corner transform into another CFG G' with no right recursion. Given an optionally arc-eager attachment strategy, this allows the parser to clear completed parse constituents from the set of incomplete constituents in working memory much earlier than with a conventional syntactic structure. The right-corner transform operates deterministically over a CFG following three mapping rules:

$$\frac{c_\eta \rightarrow c_{\eta 0}\ c_{\eta 1} \in G}{c_\eta / c_{\eta 1} \rightarrow c_{\eta 0} \in G'} \tag{1}$$

$$\frac{c_{\eta\iota} \rightarrow c_{\eta\iota 0}\ c_{\eta\iota 1} \in G,\ \ c_\eta \in C}{c_\eta / c_{\eta\iota 1} \rightarrow c_\eta / c_{\eta\iota}\ c_{\eta\iota 0} \in G'} \tag{2}$$

$$\frac{c_{\eta\iota} \rightarrow x_{\eta\iota} \in G,\ \ c_\eta \in C}{c_\eta \rightarrow c_\eta / c_{\eta\iota}\ c_{\eta\iota} \in G'} \tag{3}$$

A bottom-up incremental parsing strategy combined with the way the right-corner transform pulls each subtree into a left-expanding hierarchy ensures at most a single expansion (push) will occur at any given observation. That is, each new observation will be the leftmost leaf of a right-expanding subtree. Additionally, by reducing multiply right-branching subtrees to single rightward branches, the transform also ensures that at most a single reduction (pop) will take place at any given observation.

Schuler et al. (2010) show near complete coverage of the Wall Street Journal portion of the Penn Treebank (Marcus et al., 1993) can be achieved with a right-corner incremental parsing strategy using no more than four incomplete contituents (deferred processes), in line with recent estimates of human working memory capacity (Cowan, 2001).

Section 3 will show that, in addition to being desirable for bounded working memory restrictions, the single expansion/reduction guarantee reduces the search space between words to only two decision points — whether to expand and whether to reduce. This allows rapid processing of each candidate parse within a sequence modelling framework.

2.3 Model Formulation

This transform is then extended to PCFGs and integrated into a sequence model parser. Training on an annotated corpus yields the probability of any given syntactic state executing an expansion (creating a syntactic subtree) or a reduction (completing a syntactic subtree) to transition from every sufficiently probable (in this sense *active*) hypothesis in the working memory store.

The probability of the most likely sequence of store states $\hat{q}^{1..D}_{1..T}$ can then be defined as the product of nonterminal θ_Q, preterminal $\theta_{P,d}$, and terminal θ_X factors:

$$\hat{q}^{1..D}_{1..T} \stackrel{\text{def}}{=} \underset{q^{1..D}_{1..T}}{\text{argmax}} \prod_{t=1}^{T} \mathsf{P}_{\theta_Q}(q^{1..D}_t \mid q^{1..D}_{t\text{-}1}\ p_{t\text{-}1}) \cdot \mathsf{P}_{\theta_{P,d'}}(p_t \mid b^{d'}_t) \cdot \mathsf{P}_{\theta_X}(x_t \mid p_t) \tag{4}$$

where all incomplete constituents q^d_t are factored into active a^d_t and awaited b^d_t components:

$$q^d_t \stackrel{\text{def}}{=} a^d_t / b^d_t \tag{5}$$

and d' determines the deepest non-empty incomplete constituent of $q^{1..D}_t$:

$$d' \stackrel{\text{def}}{=} max\{d \mid q_t^d \neq \text{`–'}\} \quad (6)$$

The preterminal model $\theta_{P,d}$ denotes the expectation of a subtree containing a given preterminal, expressed in terms of side- and depth-specific grammar rules $\mathsf{P}_{\theta_{Gs,d}}(c_\eta \rightarrow c_{\eta 0}\ c_{\eta 1})$ and expected counts of left progeny categories $\mathsf{E}_{\theta_{G^*,d}}(c_\eta \xrightarrow{*} c_{\eta\iota}\ ...)$ (see Appendix A):

$$\mathsf{P}_{\theta_{P,d}}(c_{\eta\iota} \mid c_\eta) \stackrel{\text{def}}{=} \mathsf{E}_{\theta_{G^*,d}}(c_\eta \xrightarrow{*} c_{\eta\iota}\ ...) \cdot \sum_{x_{\eta\iota}} \mathsf{P}_{\theta_{GL,d}}(c_{\eta\iota} \rightarrow x_{\eta\iota}) \quad (7)$$

and the terminal model θ_X is simply:

$$\mathsf{P}_{\theta_X}(x_\eta \mid c_\eta) \stackrel{\text{def}}{=} \frac{\mathsf{P}_{\theta_G}(c_\eta \rightarrow x_\eta)}{\sum_{x_\eta} \mathsf{P}_{\theta_G}(c_\eta \rightarrow x_\eta)} \quad (8)$$

The Schuler (2009) nonterminal model θ_Q is computed from a depth-specific store element model $\theta_{Q,d}$ and a large final state model $\theta_{F,d}$:

$$\mathsf{P}_{\theta_Q}(q_t^{1..D} \mid q_{t-1}^{1..D}\ p_{t-1}) \stackrel{\text{def}}{=} \sum_{f_t^{1..D}} \prod_{d=1}^{D} \mathsf{P}_{\theta_{F,d}}(f_t^d \mid f_t^{d+1}\ q_{t-1}^d\ q_{t-1}^{d-1}) \cdot \mathsf{P}_{\theta_{Q,d}}(q_t^d \mid f_t^{d+1}\ f_t^d\ q_{t-1}^d\ q_t^{d-1}) \quad (9)$$

After each time step t and depth d, θ_Q generates a set of final states to generate a new incomplete constituent q_t^d. These final states f_t^d are factored into categories $c_{f_t^d}$ and boolean variables (0 or 1) encoding whether a reduction has taken place at depth d and time step t. The depth-specific final state model $\theta_{F,d}$ gives the probability of generating a final state f_t^d from the preceding q_t^d and q_t^{d-1} which is the probability of executing a reduction or consolidation of those incomplete constituents:

$$\mathsf{P}_{\theta_{F,d}}(f_t^d \mid f_t^{d+1}\ q_{t-1}^d\ q_{t-1}^{d-1}) \stackrel{\text{def}}{=} \begin{cases} \text{if } f_t^{d+1} = \text{`–'} : [\![f_t^d = 0]\!] \\ \text{if } f_t^{d+1} \neq \text{`–'} : \mathsf{P}_{\theta_{F,d,R}}(f_t^d \mid q_{t-1}^d\ q_{t-1}^{d-1}) \end{cases} \quad (10)$$

With these depth-specific f_t^d in hand, the model can calculate the probabilities of each possible q_t^d for each d and t based largely on the probability of transitions ($\theta_{Q,d,T}$) and expansions ($\theta_{Q,d,E}$) from the incomplete constituents at the previous time step:

$$\mathsf{P}_{\theta_{Q,d}}(q_t^d \mid f_t^{d+1}\ f_t^d\ q_{t-1}^d\ q_{t-1}^{d-1}) \stackrel{\text{def}}{=} \begin{cases} \text{if } f_t^{d+1} = \text{`–'}, f_t^d = \text{`–'} : [\![q_t^d = q_{t-1}^d]\!] \\ \text{if } f_t^{d+1} \neq \text{`–'}, f_t^d = \text{`–'} : \mathsf{P}_{\theta_{Q,d,T}}(q_t^d \mid f_t^{d+1}\ f_t^d\ q_{t-1}^d\ q_t^{d-1}) \\ \text{if } f_t^{d+1} \neq \text{`–'}, f_t^d \neq \text{`–'} : \mathsf{P}_{\theta_{Q,d,E}}(q_t^d \mid q_t^{d-1}) \end{cases} \quad (11)$$

This model is shown graphically in Figure 1.

The probability distributions over reductions ($\theta_{F,d,R}$), transitions ($\theta_{Q,d,T}$) and expansions ($\theta_{Q,d,E}$) are then defined, also in terms of side- and depth-specific grammar rules $\mathsf{P}_{\theta_{Gs,d}}(c_\eta \rightarrow c_{\eta 0}\ c_{\eta 1})$ and expected counts of left progeny categories $\mathsf{E}_{\theta_{G^*,d}}(c_\eta \xrightarrow{*} c_{\eta\iota}\ ...)$ (see Appendix A):

$$\mathsf{P}_{\theta_{Q,d,T}}(q_t^d \mid f_t^{d+1} f_t^d\ q_{t-1}^d q_t^{d-1}) \stackrel{\text{def}}{=} \begin{cases} \text{if } f_t^d \neq \text{`–'} : \mathsf{P}_{\theta_{Q,d,A}}(q_t^d \mid q_t^{d-1}\ f_t^d) \\ \text{if } f_t^d = \text{`–'} : \mathsf{P}_{\theta_{Q,d,B}}(q_t^d \mid q_{t-1}^d f_t^{d+1}) \end{cases} \quad (12)$$

$$\mathsf{P}_{\theta_{F,d,R}}(f_t^d \mid f_t^{d+1} q_{t-1}^d q_{t-1}^{d-1}) \stackrel{\text{def}}{=} \begin{cases} \text{if } c_{f_t^{d+1}} \neq x_t : [\![f_t^d = \text{`–'}]\!] \\ \text{if } c_{f_t^{d+1}} = x_t : \mathsf{P}_{\theta_{F,d,R}}(f_t^d \mid q_{t-1}^d q_{t-1}^{d-1}) \end{cases} \quad (13)$$

$$\mathsf{P}_{\theta_{Q,d,E}}(c_{\eta\iota}/c'_{\eta\iota} \mid \text{-}/c_\eta) \stackrel{\text{def}}{=} \mathsf{E}_{\theta_{G^*,d}}(c_\eta \xrightarrow{*} c_{\eta\iota}\ ...) \cdot [\![x_{\eta\iota} = c'_{\eta\iota} = c_{\eta\iota}]\!] \quad (14)$$

The subcomponent models are obtained by applying the transform rules to all possible trees proportionately to their probabilities and marginalizing over all constituents that are not used in the models:

- for active transitions (from Transform Rule 1):

$$\mathsf{P}_{\theta_{Q,d,A}}(c_{\eta\iota}/c_{\eta\iota 1} \mid \text{-}/c_\eta\ c_{\eta\iota 0}) \stackrel{\text{def}}{=} \frac{\mathsf{E}_{\theta_{G^*,d}}(c_\eta \xrightarrow{*} c_{\eta\iota}\ ...) \cdot \mathsf{P}_{\theta_{GL,d}}(c_{\eta\iota} \rightarrow c_{\eta\iota 0}\ c_{\eta\iota 1})}{\mathsf{E}_{\theta_{G^*,d}}(c_\eta \xrightarrow{+} c_{\eta\iota 0}\ ...)} \quad (15)$$

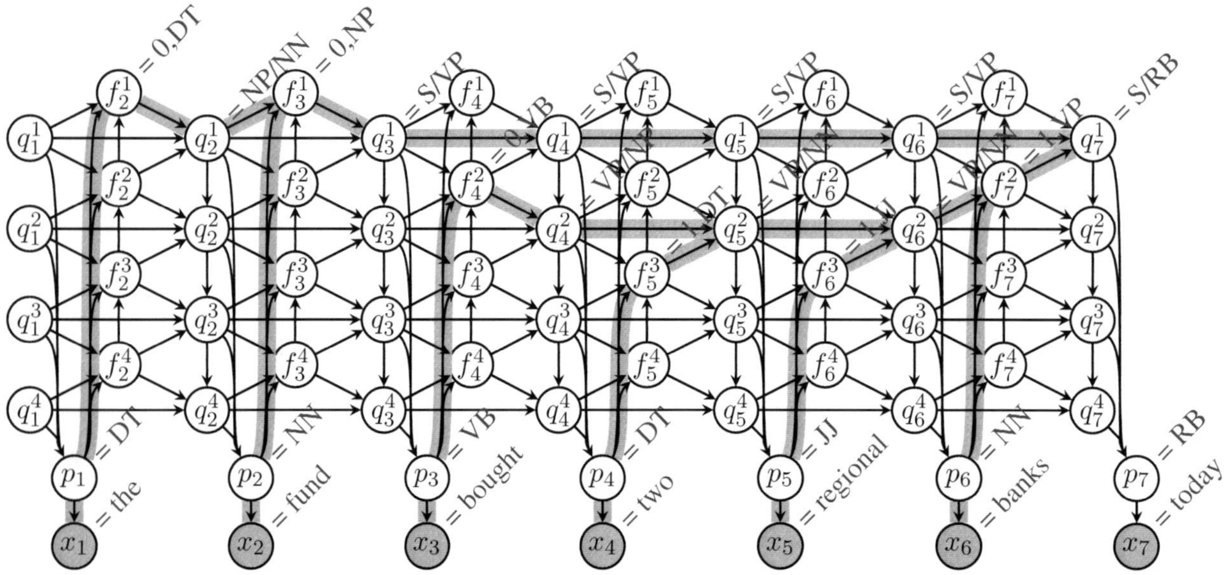

Figure 1: Schuler (2009) Sequence Model

- for awaited transitions (Transform Rule 2):

$$\mathsf{P}_{\theta_{Q,d,B}}(c_\eta/c_{\eta\iota} \mid c'_\eta/c_{\eta\iota}\; c_{\eta\iota 0}) \stackrel{\text{def}}{=} [\![c_\eta = c'_\eta]\!] \cdot \frac{\mathsf{P}_{\theta_{GR,d}}(c_{\eta\iota} \rightarrow c_{\eta\iota 0}\; c_{\eta\iota 1})}{\mathsf{E}_{\theta_{G^*,d}}(c_{\eta\iota} \xrightarrow{0} c_{\eta\iota 0}\; ...)} \tag{16}$$

- for reductions (from Transform Rule 3):

$$\mathsf{P}_{\theta_{F,d,R}}(c_{\eta\iota}, \mathbf{1} \mid \text{-}/c_\eta\; c'_{\eta\iota}/\text{-}) \stackrel{\text{def}}{=} [\![c_{\eta\iota} = c'_{\eta\iota}]\!] \cdot \frac{\mathsf{E}_{\theta_{G^*,d}}(c_\eta \xrightarrow{0} c_{\eta\iota}\; ...)}{\mathsf{E}_{\theta_{G^*,d}}(c_\eta \xrightarrow{*} c_{\eta\iota}\; ...)} \tag{17}$$

$$\mathsf{P}_{\theta_{F,d,R}}(c_{\eta\iota}, \mathbf{0} \mid \text{-}/c_\eta\; c'_{\eta\iota}/\text{-}) \stackrel{\text{def}}{=} [\![c_{\eta\iota} = c'_{\eta\iota}]\!] \cdot \frac{\mathsf{E}_{\theta_{G^*,d}}(c_\eta \xrightarrow{+} c_{\eta\iota}\; ...)}{\mathsf{E}_{\theta_{G^*,d}}(c_\eta \xrightarrow{*} c_{\eta\iota}\; ...)} \tag{18}$$

3 Simplified Model

As seen in the previous section, the right-corner parser of Schuler (2009) makes the center embedding depth explicit and each memory store element is modelled as a combination of an active and an awaited component. Each input can therefore either increase (during an expansion) or decrease (during a reduction) the store of incomplete constituents or it can alter the active or awaited component of the deepest incomplete constituent (the *affectable* element). Alterations of the awaited component of the affectable element can be thought of as the expansion and immediate reduction of a syntactic constituent. The grammar models transitions in the active component implicitly, so these are conceptualized as consisting of neither an expansion nor a reduction.

Removing some of the variables in this model results in one that looks much more like a neural network (McClelland and Elman, 1986; Elman, 1991; Norris, 1994; Norris and McQueen, 2008) in that all remaining variables have cognitive correllates — in particular, they correspond to incomplete constituents in working memory — while still maintaining the ability to explicitly represent phrase structure. This section will demonstrate how it is possible to exploit this to obtain a large reduction in the number of modelled random variables.

In the Schuler (2009) sequence model, eight random variables are used to model the hidden states at each time step (see Figure 1). Half of these variables are *joint* consisting of two further (active and awaited) constituent variables, while the other half are merely over intermediate *final* states. Although the entire store is carried from time step to time step, only one memory element is affectable at any one time, and this element may be reduced zero or one times (using an intermediate final state), and expanded zero or one times (using an incomplete constituent state), yielding four possible combinations. This means the model only actually needs one of its intermediate final states.

The transition model θ_Q can therefore be simplified with terms $\theta_{F,d}$ for the probability of expanding the incomplete constituent at d, and terms $\theta_{A,d}$ and $\theta_{B,d}$ for reducing the resulting constituent (defining the active and awaited components of a new incomplete constituent), along with terms for copying incomplete constituents above this affectable element, and for emptying the elements below it:

$$\begin{aligned}
&\mathsf{P}_{\theta_Q}(q_t^{1..D} \mid q_{t-1}^{1..D}\ p_{t-1}) \\
&\stackrel{\text{def}}{=} \mathsf{P}_{\theta_{F,d'}}(\text{`+'} \mid b_{t-1}^{d'}\ p_{t-1}) \cdot \mathsf{P}_{\theta_{A,d'}}(\text{`}-\text{'} \mid b_{t-1}^{d'-1}\ a_{t-1}^{d'}) \\
&\quad \cdot [\![a_t^{d'-1} = a_{t-1}^{d'-1}]\!] \cdot \mathsf{P}_{\theta_{B,d'-1}}(b_t^{d'-1} \mid b_{t-1}^{d'-1}\ a_{t-1}^{d'}) \\
&\quad \cdot [\![q_t^{1..d'-2} = q_{t-1}^{1..d'-2}]\!] \cdot [\![q_t^{d'..D} = \text{`}-\text{'}]\!] \\
&+ \mathsf{P}_{\theta_{F,d'}}(\text{`+'} \mid b_{t-1}^{d'}\ p_{t-1}) \cdot \mathsf{P}_{\theta_{A,d'}}(a_t^{d'} \mid b_{t-1}^{d'-1}\ a_{t-1}^{d'}) \\
&\quad \cdot \mathsf{P}_{\theta_{B,d'}}(b_t^{d'} \mid a_t^{d'}\ a_{t-1}^{d'+1}) \\
&\quad \cdot [\![q_t^{1..d'-1} = q_{t-1}^{1..d'-1}]\!] \cdot [\![q_t^{d'+1..D} = \text{`}-\text{'}]\!] \\
&+ \mathsf{P}_{\theta_{F,d'}}(\text{`}-\text{'} \mid b_{t-1}^{d'}\ p_{t-1}) \cdot \mathsf{P}_{\theta_{A,d'}}(\text{`}-\text{'} \mid b_{t-1}^{d'}\ p_{t-1}) \\
&\quad \cdot [\![a_t^{d'} = a_{t-1}^{d'}]\!] \cdot \mathsf{P}_{\theta_{B,d'}}(b_t^{d'} \mid b_{t-1}^{d'}\ p_{t-1}) \\
&\quad \cdot [\![q_t^{1..d'-1} = q_{t-1}^{1..d'-1}]\!] \cdot [\![q_t^{d'+1..D} = \text{`}-\text{'}]\!] \\
&+ \mathsf{P}_{\theta_{F,d'}}(\text{`}-\text{'} \mid b_{t-1}^{d'}\ p_{t-1}) \cdot \mathsf{P}_{\theta_{A,d'}}(a_t^{d'+1} \mid b_{t-1}^{d'}\ p_{t-1}) \\
&\quad \cdot \mathsf{P}_{\theta_{B,d'}}(b_t^{d'+1} \mid a_t^{d'+1}\ p_{t-1}) \\
&\quad \cdot [\![q_t^{1..d'} = q_{t-1}^{1..d'}]\!] \cdot [\![q_t^{d'+2..D} = \text{`}-\text{'}]\!]
\end{aligned} \tag{19}$$

The first element of the sum in Equation 19 computes the probability of a reduction with no expansion (decreasing d'). The second corresponds to the probability of a store undergoing neither an expansion nor a reduction (a transition to a new active constituent at the same embedding depth). In the third is the probability of an expansion and a reduction (a transition among awaited constituents at the same embedding depth). Finally, the last term yields the probability of an expansion without a reduction (increasing d').

From Equation 19 it may be seen that the unaffected store elements of each time step are maintained sans change as guaranteed by the single-reduction feature of the right-corner parser. This results in a large representational economy by making the majority of store state decisions deterministic. This representational economy will later translate into computational efficiencies (see section 5). In this sense, cognitive modelling contributes to a practical speed increase.

Since the bulk of the state remains the same, the recognizer can access the affectable variable and operate solely over the transition possibilities from that variable to calculate the distribution over store states for the next time step to explore. Reflecting this change, the hidden states now model a single final-state variable (f) for results of the expansion decision, and the affectable variable resulting from the reduction decision (both its active (a) and awaited (b) categories), as well as the preterminal state (p) defined in the previous section. These models are again expressed in terms of side- and depth-specific grammar rules $\mathsf{P}_{\theta_{Gs,d}}(c_\eta \rightarrow c_{\eta 0}\ c_{\eta 1})$ and expected counts of left progeny categories $\mathsf{E}_{\theta_{G^*,d}}(c_\eta \xrightarrow{*} c_{\eta\iota}\ ...)$ (see Appendix A).

Expansion probabilities are modelled as a binary decision depending on whether or not the awaited component of the affectable variable c_η is likely to expand immediately into an anticipated preterminal $c_{\eta\iota}$ (resulting in a non-empty final state: '+') or if intervening embeddings are necessary given the affectable active component (yielding no final state: '–'):

$$\mathsf{P}_{\theta_{F,d}}(f \mid c_\eta\ c_{\eta\iota}) \stackrel{\text{def}}{=} \begin{cases} \text{if } f = \text{`+'} : \dfrac{\mathsf{E}_{\theta_{G^*,d}}(c_\eta \xrightarrow{0} c_{\eta\iota}\ ...)}{\mathsf{E}_{\theta_{G^*,d}}(c_\eta \xrightarrow{*} c_{\eta\iota}\ ...)} \\ \text{if } f = \text{`}-\text{'} : \dfrac{\mathsf{E}_{\theta_{G^*,d}}(c_\eta \xrightarrow{+} c_{\eta\iota}\ ...)}{\mathsf{E}_{\theta_{G^*,d}}(c_\eta \xrightarrow{*} c_{\eta\iota}\ ...)} \end{cases} \tag{20}$$

The active component category $c_{\eta\iota}$ is defined as depending on the category of the awaited component above it c_η and its left-hand child $c_{\eta\iota 0}$:

$$\begin{aligned}
\mathsf{P}_{\theta_{A,d}}(c_{\eta\iota} \mid c_\eta\ c_{\eta\iota 0}) &\stackrel{\text{def}}{=} \frac{\mathsf{E}_{\theta_{G^*,d}}(c_\eta \xrightarrow{1} c_{\eta\iota 0}\ ...)}{\mathsf{E}_{\theta_{G^*,d}}(c_\eta \xrightarrow{+} c_{\eta\iota 0}\ ...)} \cdot [\![c_{\eta\iota} = \text{`}-\text{'}]\!] \\
&+ \frac{\mathsf{E}_{\theta_{G^*,d}}(c_\eta \xrightarrow{+} c_{\eta\iota}\ ...) \cdot \mathsf{P}_{\theta_{GL,d}}(c_{\eta\iota} \rightarrow c_{\eta\iota 0}\ ...)}{\mathsf{E}_{\theta_{G^*,d}}(c_\eta \xrightarrow{+} c_{\eta\iota 0}\ ...)}
\end{aligned} \tag{21}$$

The awaited component category $c_{\eta 1}$ is defined as

depending on the category of its parent c_η and the preceding sibling $c_{\eta 0}$:

$$\mathsf{P}_{\theta_{B,d}}(c_{\eta 1} \mid c_\eta \, c_{\eta 0}) \stackrel{\text{def}}{=} \frac{\mathsf{P}_{\theta_{GR,d}}(c_\eta \rightarrow c_{\eta 0} \; c_{\eta 1})}{\mathsf{E}_{\theta_{G^*,d}}(c_\eta \xrightarrow{1} c_{\eta 0} \; ...)} \tag{22}$$

Both of these make sense given the manner in which the right-corner parser shifts dependencies to the left down the tree in order to obtain incremental information about upcoming constituents.

3.1 Graphical Representation

In order to be represented graphically, the working memory store θ_Q is factored into a single expansion term θ_F and a product of depth-specific reduction terms $\theta_{Q,d}$:

$$\begin{aligned}\mathsf{P}_{\theta_Q}(q_t^{1..D} \mid q_{t-1}^{1..D} \, p_{t-1}) \stackrel{\text{def}}{=} & \sum_{f_t} \mathsf{P}_{\theta_F}(f_t \mid q_{t-1}^{1..D}) \\ & \cdot \prod_{d=1}^{D} \mathsf{P}_{\theta_{Q,d}}(q_t^d \mid q_{t-1}^{1..D} \, p_{t-1} \, f_t \, q_t^{d+1})\end{aligned} \tag{23}$$

and the depth-specific reduction model $\theta_{Q,d}$ is factored into individual decisions over each random variable:

$$\mathsf{P}_{\theta_{Q,d}}(q_t^d \mid q_{t-1}^{1..D} \, p_{t-1} \, f_t \, q_t^{d+1}) \stackrel{\text{def}}{=}$$
$$\begin{cases} \text{if } q_t^{d+1} = \text{`–'}, f_t \neq \text{`–'}, d = d'-1 : \\ \qquad [\![a_t^d = a_{t-1}^d]\!] \cdot \mathsf{P}_{\theta_{B,d}}(b_t^d \mid b_{t-1}^d \, a_{t-1}^{d+1}) \\ \text{if } q_t^{d+1} = \text{`–'}, f_t \neq \text{`–'}, d = d' : \\ \qquad \mathsf{P}_{\theta_{A,d}}(a_t^d \mid b_{t-1}^{d-1} \, a_{t-1}^d) \cdot \mathsf{P}_{\theta_{B,d}}(b_t^d \mid a_t^d \, a_{t-1}^d) \\ \text{if } q_t^{d+1} = \text{`–'}, f_t = \text{`–'}, d = d' : \\ \qquad [\![a_t^d = a_{t-1}^d]\!] \cdot \mathsf{P}_{\theta_{B,d}}(b_t^d \mid b_{t-1}^d \, p_{t-1}) \\ \text{if } q_t^{d+1} = \text{`–'}, f_t = \text{`–'}, d = d'+1 : \\ \qquad \mathsf{P}_{\theta_{A,d}}(a_t^d \mid b_{t-1}^{d-1} \, p_{t-1}) \cdot \mathsf{P}_{\theta_{B,d}}(b_t^d \mid a_t^d \, p_{t-1}) \\ \text{if } q_t^{d+1} \neq \text{`–'} : [\![q_t^d = q_{t-1}^d]\!] \\ \text{otherwise} : [\![q_t^d = \text{`–'}]\!] \end{cases} \tag{24}$$

This dependency structure is represented graphically in Figure 2.

The first conditional in Equation 24 checks whether the input causes a reduction but no expansion (completing a subtree parse). In this case, d' is reduced from the previous t, and the relevant q_{t-1}^d is copied to q_t^d except the awaited constituent is altered to reflect the completion of its preceding awaited subtree. In the second case, the parser makes an active transition as it completes a left subtree and begins exploring the right subtree. The third case is similar to the first except it transitions between two like depths (awaited transition), and depends on the preterminal just seen to contrive a new subtree to explore. In the fourth case, d' is incremented as another incomplete constituent opens up in working memory. The final two cases simply update the unaffected store states to reflect their previous states at time $t-1$.

4 Discussion

This factoring of redundant hidden states out of the Schuler (2009) probabilistic sequence model shows that cognitive modelling can more closely approximate a simple recurrent network model of language processing (Elman, 1991). Probabilistic sequence model parsers have previously been modelled with random variables over incomplete constituents (Schuler, 2009). In the current implementation, each variable can be thought of as a bank of artificial neurons. These artificial neurons inhibit one another through the process of normalization. Conversely, they activate artificial neurons at subsequent time steps by contributing probability mass through the transformed grammar. This point was made by Norris and McQueen (2008) with respect to lexical access; this model extends it to parsing.

Recurrent networks can parse simple sentences but run into problems when running over more complex datasets. This limitation comes from the unsupervised methods typically used to train them, which have difficulty scaling to sufficiently large training sets for more complex constructions. The approach described in this paper uses a hidden context similar to that of a recurrent network to inform the progression of the parse, except that the context is in terms of random variables with distributions over a set of explicit syntactic categories. By framing the variable domains in a linguistically-motivated fashion, the problem of acquisition can be divested from the problem of processing. This paper then uses the semi-supervised grammar training of Petrov et al. (2006) in order to develop a simple, accurate model for broad-coverage parsing independent of scale.

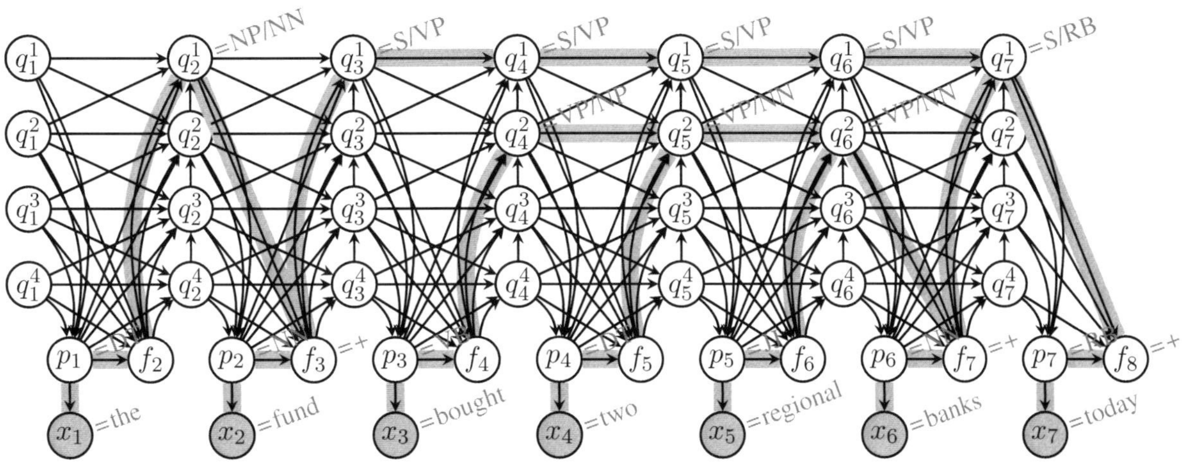

Figure 2: Parse using Simplified Model

Like Schuler (2009), the incremental parser discussed here operates in $O(n)$ time where n is the length of the input. Further, by its incremental nature, this parser is able to run continuously on a stream of input, which allows any other processes dependent on the input (such as discourse integration) to run in parallel regardless of the length of the input.

5 Computational Benefit

Due to the decreased number of decisions required by this simplified model, it is substantially faster than previous similar models. To test this speed increase, the simplified model was compared with that of Schuler (2009). Both parsers used a grammar that had undergone 5 iterations of the Petrov et al. (2006) split-merge-smooth algorithm as found to be optimal by Petrov and Klein (2007), and both used a beam-width of 500 elements. Sections 02-21 of the Wall Street Journal Treebank were used in training the grammar induction for both parsers according to Petrov et al. (2006), and Section 23 was used for evaluation. No tuning was done as part of the transform to a sequence model. Speed results can be seen in Table 1. While the speed is not state-of-the-art in the field of parsing at large, it does break new ground for factored sequence model parsers.

To test the accuracy of this parser, it was compared using varying beam-widths to the Petrov and Klein (2007) and Roark (2001) parsers. With the exception of the Roark (2001) parser, all parsers used 5 iterations of the Petrov et al. (2006) split-merge-smooth algorithm, and the training and testing datasets remained the same. These results may be seen in Table 2. Note that the Petrov and Klein (2007) parser allows unary branching within the phrase structure, which is not well-defined under the right-corner transform. To obtain a fair comparison, it was also run with strict binarization. The current approach achieves comparable accuracy to the Petrov and Klein (2007) parser assuming a strictly binary-branching phrase structure.

System	Sec/Sent
Schuler 2009	74
Current Model	12

Table 1: Speed comparison with an unfactored probabilistic sequence model using a beam-width of 500 elements

System	P	R	F
Roark 2001	86.6	86.5	86.5
Current Model (500)	86.6	87.3	87.0
Current Model (2000)	87.8	87.8	87.8
Current Model (5000)	87.8	87.8	87.8
Petrov Klein (Binary)	88.1	87.8	88.0
Petrov Klein (+Unary)	88.3	88.6	88.5

Table 2: Accuracy comparison with state-of-the-art models. Numbers in parentheses are number of parallel activated hypotheses

6 Conclusion

The primary goal of this paper was to demonstrate that a cognitively-motivated factoring of an existing probabilistic sequence model parser (Schuler, 2009) is not only more attractive from a modelling perspective but also more efficient. Such factoring yields a much slimmer model where every variable has cognitive correlates to working memory elements. This also renders several transition probabilities deterministic and the ensuing representational economy leads to a 5-fold increase in parsing speed. The results shown here suggest cognitive modelling can lead to computational benefits.

References

Alfred V. Aho and Jeffery D. Ullman. 1972. *The Theory of Parsing, Translation and Compiling; Volume. I: Parsing*. Prentice-Hall, Englewood Cliffs, New Jersey.

P. D. Allopenna, J. S. Magnuson, and M. K. Tanenhaus. 1998. Tracking the time course of spoken word recognition using eye movements: evidence for continuous mapping models. *Journal of Memory and Language*, 38:419–439.

G. T. M. Altmann and Y. Kamide. 1999. Incremental interpretation at verbs: restricting the domain of subsequent reference. *Cognition*, 73:247–264.

Richard Bellman. 1957. *Dynamic Programming*. Princeton University Press, Princeton, NJ.

Thomas G. Bever. 1970. The cognitive basis for linguistic structure. In J.R̃. Hayes, editor, *Cognition and the Development of Language*, pages 279–362. Wiley, New York.

Matthew Botvinick. 2007. Multilevel structure in behavior and in the brain: a computational model of fusters hierarchy. *Philosophical Transactions of the Royal Society, Series B: Biological Sciences*, 362:1615–1626.

Nelson Cowan. 2001. The magical number 4 in short-term memory: A reconsideration of mental storage capacity. *Behavioral and Brain Sciences*, 24:87–185.

Vera Demberg and Frank Keller. 2008. Data from eye-tracking corpora as evidence for theories of syntactic processing complexity. *Cognition*, 109(2):193–210.

Jeffrey L. Elman. 1991. Distributed representations, simple recurrent networks, and grammatical structure. *Machine Learning*, 7:195–225.

John Hale. 2001. A probabilistic earley parser as a psycholinguistic model. In *Proceedings of the Second Meeting of the North American Chapter of the Association for Computational Linguistics*, pages 159–166, Pittsburgh, PA.

Jonathan C Horton and Daniel L Adams. 2005. The cortical column: a structure without a function. *Philosophical Transactions of the Royal Society of London - Series B: Biological Sciences*, 360(1456):837–862.

Daniel Jurafsky. 1996. A probabilistic model of lexical and syntactic access and disambiguation. *Cognitive Science: A Multidisciplinary Journal*, 20(2):137–194.

Roger Levy. 2008. Expectation-based syntactic comprehension. *Cognition*, 106(3):1126–1177.

Mitchell P. Marcus, Beatrice Santorini, and Mary Ann Marcinkiewicz. 1993. Building a large annotated corpus of English: the Penn Treebank. *Computational Linguistics*, 19(2):313–330.

William D. Marslen-Wilson. 1975. Sentence perception as an interactive parallel process. *Science*, 189(4198):226–228.

Marshall R. Mayberry, III and Risto Miikkulainen. 2003. Incremental nonmonotonic parsing through semantic self-organization. In *Proceedings of the* 25th *Annual Conference of the Cognitive Science Society*, pages 798–803, Boston, MA.

James L. McClelland and Jeffrey L. Elman. 1986. The trace model of speech perception. *Cognitive Psychology*, 18:1–86.

Dennis Norris and James M. McQueen. 2008. Shortlist b: A bayesian model of continuous speech recognition. *Psychological Review*, 115(2):357–395.

Dennis Norris. 1994. Shortlist: A connectionist model of continuous speech recognition. *Cognition*, 52:189–234.

Slav Petrov and Dan Klein. 2007. Improved inference for unlexicalized parsing. In *Proceedings of NAACL HLT 2007*, pages 404–411, Rochester, New York, April. Association for Computational Linguistics.

Slav Petrov, Leon Barrett, Romain Thibaux, and Dan Klein. 2006. Learning accurate, compact, and interpretable tree annotation. In *Proceedings of the 44th Annual Meeting of the Association for Computational Linguistics (COLING/ACL'06)*.

Brian Roark. 2001. Probabilistic top-down parsing and language modeling. *Computational Linguistics*, 27(2):249–276.

William Schuler, Samir AbdelRahman, Tim Miller, and Lane Schwartz. 2010. Broad-coverage incremental parsing using human-like memory constraints. *Computational Linguistics*, 36(1):1–30.

William Schuler. 2009. Parsing with a bounded stack using a model-based right-corner transform. In *Proceedings of NAACL/HLT 2009*, NAACL '09, pages 344–352, Boulder, Colorado. Association for Computational Linguistics.

Michael K. Tanenhaus, Michael J. Spivey-Knowlton, Kathy M. Eberhard, and Julie E. Sedivy. 1995. Integration of visual and linguistic information in spoken language comprehension. *Science*, 268:1632–1634.

A Grammar Formulation

Given D memory elements indexed by d (see Section 2.2) and a PCFG θ_G, the probability $\theta^{(k)}_{Ts,d}$ of a tree rooted at a left or right sibling $s \in \{L, R\}$ of category $c_\eta \in C$ requiring $d \in 1..D$ memory elements is defined recursively over paths of increasing length k:

$$\mathsf{P}_{\theta^{(0)}_{Ts,d}}(1 \mid c_\eta) \stackrel{\text{def}}{=} 0 \tag{25}$$

$$\begin{aligned}\mathsf{P}_{\theta^{(k)}_{TL,d}}(1 \mid c_\eta) \stackrel{\text{def}}{=} & \sum_{x_\eta} \mathsf{P}_{\theta_G}(c_\eta \to x_\eta) \\ & + \sum_{c_{\eta 0}, c_{\eta 1}} \mathsf{P}_{\theta_G}(c_\eta \to c_{\eta 0}\ c_{\eta 1}) \\ & \cdot \mathsf{P}_{\theta^{(k-1)}_{TL,d}}(1 \mid c_{\eta 0}) \cdot \mathsf{P}_{\theta^{(k-1)}_{TR,d}}(1 \mid c_{\eta 1})\end{aligned} \tag{26}$$

$$\begin{aligned}\mathsf{P}_{\theta^{(k)}_{TR,d}}(1 \mid c_\eta) \stackrel{\text{def}}{=} & \sum_{x_\eta} \mathsf{P}_{\theta_G}(c_\eta \to x_\eta) \\ & + \sum_{c_{\eta 0}, c_{\eta 1}} \mathsf{P}_{\theta_G}(c_\eta \to c_{\eta 0}\ c_{\eta 1}) \\ & \cdot \mathsf{P}_{\theta^{(k-1)}_{TL,d+1}}(1 \mid c_{\eta 0}) \cdot \mathsf{P}_{\theta^{(k-1)}_{TR,d}}(1 \mid c_{\eta 1})\end{aligned} \tag{27}$$

Note that the center embedding depth d increases only for left children of right children. This is because in a binary branching structure, center embeddings manifest as zigzags. Since the model is also sensitive to the depth d of each decomposition, the side- and depth-specific probabilities of $\theta_{GL,d}$ and $\theta_{GR,d}$ are defined as follows:

$$\mathsf{P}_{\theta_{GL,d}}(c_\eta \to x_\eta) \stackrel{\text{def}}{=} \frac{\mathsf{P}_{\theta_G}(c_\eta \to x_\eta)}{\mathsf{P}_{\theta^{(\infty)}_{TL,d}}(1 \mid c_\eta)} \tag{28}$$

$$\mathsf{P}_{\theta_{GR,d}}(c_\eta \to x_\eta) \stackrel{\text{def}}{=} \frac{\mathsf{P}_{\theta_G}(c_\eta \to x_\eta)}{\mathsf{P}_{\theta^{(\infty)}_{TR,d}}(1 \mid c_\eta)} \tag{29}$$

$$\begin{aligned}\mathsf{P}_{\theta_{GL,d}}(c_\eta \to c_{\eta 0}\ c_{\eta 1}) \stackrel{\text{def}}{=} & \mathsf{P}_{\theta_G}(c_\eta \to c_{\eta 0}\ c_{\eta 1}) \\ & \cdot \mathsf{P}_{\theta^{(\infty)}_{TL,d}}(1 \mid c_{\eta 0}) \cdot \mathsf{P}_{\theta^{(\infty)}_{TR,d}}(1 \mid c_{\eta 1}) \\ & \cdot \mathsf{P}_{\theta^{(\infty)}_{TL,d}}(1 \mid c_\eta)^{-1}\end{aligned} \tag{30}$$

$$\begin{aligned}\mathsf{P}_{\theta_{GR,d}}(c_\eta \to c_{\eta 0}\ c_{\eta 1}) \stackrel{\text{def}}{=} & \mathsf{P}_{\theta_G}(c_\eta \to c_{\eta 0}\ c_{\eta 1}) \\ & \cdot \mathsf{P}_{\theta^{(\infty)}_{TL,d+1}}(1 \mid c_{\eta 0}) \cdot \mathsf{P}_{\theta^{(\infty)}_{TR,d}}(1 \mid c_{\eta 1}) \\ & \cdot \mathsf{P}_{\theta^{(\infty)}_{TR,d}}(1 \mid c_\eta)^{-1}\end{aligned} \tag{31}$$

The model will also need an expected count $\mathsf{E}_{\theta_{G^*,d}}(c_\eta \stackrel{*}{\to} c_{\eta\iota}\ ...)$ of the given child constituent $c_{\eta\iota}$ dominating a prefix of constituent c_η. Expected versions of these counts may later be used to derive probabilities of memory store state transitions (see Sections 2.3, 3).

$$\mathsf{E}_{\theta_{G^*,d}}(c_\eta \stackrel{0}{\to} c_\eta\ ...) \stackrel{\text{def}}{=} \sum_{x_\eta} \mathsf{P}_{\theta_{GR,d}}(c_\eta \to x_\eta) \tag{32}$$

$$\mathsf{E}_{\theta_{G^*,d}}(c_\eta \stackrel{1}{\to} c_{\eta 0}\ ...) \stackrel{\text{def}}{=} \sum_{c_{\eta 1}} \mathsf{P}_{\theta_{GR,d}}(c_\eta \to c_{\eta 0}\ c_{\eta 1}) \tag{33}$$

$$\begin{aligned}\mathsf{E}_{\theta_{G^*,d}}(c_\eta \stackrel{k}{\to} c_{\eta\iota 0}\ ...) \stackrel{\text{def}}{=} & \sum_{c_{\eta\iota}} \mathsf{E}_{\theta_{G^*,d}}(c_\eta \stackrel{k-1}{\to} c_{\eta\iota}\ ...) \\ & \cdot \sum_{c_{\eta\iota 1}} \mathsf{P}_{\theta_{GL,d}}(c_{\eta\iota} \to c_{\eta\iota 0}\ c_{\eta\iota 1})\end{aligned} \tag{34}$$

$$\mathsf{E}_{\theta_{G^*,d}}(c_\eta \stackrel{*}{\to} c_{\eta\iota}\ ...) \stackrel{\text{def}}{=} \sum_{k=0}^{\infty} \mathsf{E}_{\theta_{G^*,d}}(c_\eta \stackrel{k}{\to} c_{\eta\iota}\ ...) \tag{35}$$

$$\mathsf{E}_{\theta_{G^*,d}}(c_\eta \stackrel{+}{\to} c_{\eta\iota}\ ...) \stackrel{\text{def}}{=} \sum_{k=1}^{\infty} \mathsf{E}_{\theta_{G^*,d}}(c_\eta \stackrel{k}{\to} c_{\eta\iota}\ ...) \tag{36}$$

Equation 32 gives the probability of a constituent appearing as an observation, and Equation 33 gives the probability of a constituent appearing as a left child. Equation 34 extends the previous two equations to account for a constituent appearing at an arbitrarily deep embedded path of length k. Taking the sum of all k path lengths (as in Equation 35) allows the model to account for constituents anywhere in the left progeny of the dominated subtree. Similarly, Equation 36 gives the expectation that the constituent is non-immediately dominated by c_η. In practice the infinite sum is estimated to some constant K using value iteration (Bellman, 1957).

Sequential vs. Hierarchical Syntactic Models of Human Incremental Sentence Processing

Victoria Fossum and Roger Levy
Department of Linguistics
University of California, San Diego
9500 Gilman Dr.
La Jolla, CA 92093
{vfossum, rlevy}@ucsd.edu

Abstract

Experimental evidence demonstrates that syntactic structure influences human online sentence processing behavior. Despite this evidence, open questions remain: which type of syntactic structure best explains observed behavior–hierarchical or sequential, and lexicalized or unlexicalized? Recently, Frank and Bod (2011) find that unlexicalized sequential models predict reading times better than unlexicalized hierarchical models, relative to a baseline prediction model that takes word-level factors into account. They conclude that the human parser is insensitive to hierarchical syntactic structure. We investigate these claims and find a picture more complicated than the one they present. First, we show that incorporating additional lexical n-gram probabilities estimated from several different corpora into the baseline model of Frank and Bod (2011) eliminates all differences in accuracy between those unlexicalized sequential and hierarchical models. Second, we show that lexicalizing the hierarchical models used in Frank and Bod (2011) significantly improves prediction accuracy relative to the unlexicalized versions. Third, we show that using state-of-the-art lexicalized hierarchical models further improves prediction accuracy. Our results demonstrate that the claim of Frank and Bod (2011) that sequential models predict reading times better than hierarchical models is premature, and also that lexicalization matters for prediction accuracy.

1 Introduction

Various factors influence human reading times during online sentence processing, including word-level factors such as word length, unigram and bigram probabilities, and position in the sentence. Yet word-level factors cannot explain many observed processing phenomena; ample experimental evidence exists for the influence of syntax on human behavior during online sentence processing, beyond what can be predicted using word-level factors alone. Examples include the English subject/object relative clause asymmetry (Gibson et al., 2005; King and Just, 1991) and anti-locality effects in German (Konieczny, 2000; Konieczny and Döring, 2003), Hindi (Vasishth and Lewis, 2006), and Japanese (Nakatani and Gibson, 2008). Levy (2008) shows that these processing phenomena can be explained by surprisal theory under a hierarchical probabilistic context-free grammar (PCFG). Other evidence of syntactic expectation in sentence processing includes the facilitation of processing at "or" following "either" (Staub and Clifton, 2006); expectations of heavy noun phrase shifts (Staub et al., 2006); ellipsis processing (Lau et al., 2006); and syntactic priming (Sturt et al., 2010).

Experimental evidence for the influence of syntax on human behavior is not limited to experiments carefully designed to isolate a particular processing phenomenon. Several broad-coverage experimental studies have shown that surprisal under hierarchical syntactic models predicts human processing difficulty on large corpora of naturally occurring text, even after word-level factors have been taken into account (Boston et al., 2008; Demberg and Keller, 2008; Roark et al., 2009).

Despite this evidence, in recent work Frank and Bod (2011) challenge the notion that hierarchical syntactic structure is strictly necessary to predict reading times. They compare per-word surprisal predictions from unlexicalized hierarchical and sequential models of syntactic structure along two axes: *linguistic accuracy* (how well the model predicts the test corpus) and *psychological accuracy* (how well the model predicts observed reading times on the test corpus). They find that, while hierarchical phrase-structure grammars (PSG's) achieve better linguistic accuracy, sequential echo state networks (ESN's) achieve better psychological accuracy on the English Dundee corpus (Kennedy and Pynte, 2005). Frank and Bod (2011) do not include lexicalized syntactic models in the comparison on the grounds that, once word-level factors have been included as control predictors in the reading times model, lexicalized syntactic models do not predict reading times better than unlexicalized syntactic models (Demberg and Keller, 2008). Based on the results of their comparisons between unlexicalized models, they conclude that the human parser is insensitive to hierarchical syntactic structure.

In light of the existing evidence that hierarchical syntax influences human sentence processing, the claim of Frank and Bod (2011) is surprising. In this work, we investigate this claim, and find a picture more complicated than the one they present. We first replicate the results of Frank and Bod (2011) using the dataset provided by the authors, verifying that we obtain the same linguistic and psychological accuracies reported by the authors. We then extend their work in several ways. First, we repeat their comparisons using additional, more robustly estimated lexical n-gram probabilities as control predictors in the baseline model.[1] We show that when these additional lexical n-gram probabilities are used as control predictors, any differences in psychological accuracy between the hierarchical and sequential models used in Frank and Bod (2011) vanish. Second, while they restrict their comparisons to unlexicalized models over part-of-speech (POS) tags, we investigate the lexicalized versions of each hierarchical model, and show that lexicalization significantly improves psychological accuracy. Third, while they explore only a subset of the PSG's implemented under the incremental parser of Roark (2001), we explore a state-of-the-art lexicalized hierarchical model that conditions on richer contexts, and show that this model performs still better. Our findings demonstrate that Frank and Bod (2011)'s strong claim that sequential models predict reading times better than hierarchical models is premature, and also that lexicalization improves the psychological accuracy of hierarchical models.

2 Related Work

Several broad-coverage experimental studies demonstrate that surprisal under a hierarchical syntactic model predicts human processing difficulty on a corpus of naturally occurring text, even after word-level factors have been taken into account. Under surprisal theory (Hale, 2001; Levy, 2008), processing difficulty at word w_i is proportional to reading time at w_i, which in turn is proportional to the surprisal of w_i in the context in which it is observed: $surprisal(w_i) = -log(pr(w_i|context))$. Typically, $context \approx w_1...w_{i-1}$. Computing $surprisal(w_i)$ thus reduces to computing $-log(pr(w_i|w_1...wi - 1))$. Henceforth, we refer to this original formulation of surprisal as *total surprisal*.

Boston et al. (2008) show that surprisal estimates from a lexicalized dependency parser (Nivre, 2006) and an unlexicalized PCFG are significant predictors of reading times on the German Potsdam Corpus. Demberg and Keller (2008) propose to isolate syntactic surprisal from total surprisal by replacing each word with its POS tag, then calculating surprisal as usual under the incremental probabilistic phrase-structure parser of Roark (2001). (Following Roark et al. (2009), we hereafter refer to this type of surprisal as *POS surprisal*.) They find that only POS surprisal, not total surprisal, is a significant predictor of reading time predictions on the English Dundee corpus.

Demberg and Keller (2008)'s definition of POS surprisal introduces two constraints. First, by omit-

[1]By *robustly estimated*, we mean that these probabilities are estimated from larger corpora and use a better smoothing method (Kneser-Ney) than the lexical n-grams of Frank and Bod (2011).

ting lexical information from the conditioning context, they ignore differences among words within a syntactic category that can influence syntactic expectations about upcoming material. Second, by replacing words with their most likely POS tags, they treat POS tags as veridical, observed input rather than marginalizing over all possible latent POS tag sequences consistent with the observed words.

Roark et al. (2009) propose a more principled way of decomposing total surprisal into its syntactic and lexical components, defining the syntactic surprisal of w_i as:

$$-log\frac{\sum_{D:yield(D)=w_1...w_i} pr(D\ minus\ last\ step)}{\sum_{D:yield(D)=w_1...w_{i-1}} pr(D)}$$

and the lexical surprisal of w_i as:

$$-log\frac{\sum_{D:yield(D)=w_1...w_i} pr(D)}{\sum_{D:yield(D)=w_1...w_i} pr(D\ minus\ last\ step)}$$

where D is the set of derivations in the parser's beam at any given point; $D : yield(D) = w_1...w_i$ is the set of all derivations in D consistent with $w_1...w_i$; and $D\ minus\ last\ step$ includes all steps in the derivation *except* for the last step, in which w_i is generated by conditioning upon all previous steps of D (including t_i).

Roark et al. (2009) show that syntactic surprisal produces more accurate reading time predictions on an English corpus than POS surprisal, and that decomposing total surprisal into its syntactic and lexical components produces more accurate reading time predictions than total surprisal taken as a single quantity. In this work, we compare not only different types of syntactic models, but also different measures of surprisal under each of those models (total, POS, syntactic-only, and lexical-only).

3 Models

Estimating $surprisal(w_i)$ amounts to calculating $-log(pr(w_i|w_1...w_{i-1}))$. Language models differ in the way they estimate the conditional probability of the event w_i given the observed context $w_1...w_{i-1}$. In the traditional formulation of surprisal under a hierarchical model, the event w_i is conditioned not only on the *observed* context $w_1...w_{i-1}$ but also on the *latent* context consisting of the syntactic trees T whose yield is $w_1...w_{i-1}$; computing $pr(w_i|w_1...w_{i-1})$ therefore requires marginalizing over all possible latent contexts T. In this formulation of surprisal, the context includes lexical information ($w_1...w_{i-1}$) as well as syntactic information ($T : yield(T) = w_1...w_{i-1}$), and the predicted event itself (w_i) contains lexical information.

Other formulations of surprisal are also possible, in which the event, observed context, and latent context are otherwise defined. In this work, we classify syntactic models as follows: *lexicalized* models include lexical information in the context, in the predicted event, or both; *unlexicalized* models include lexical information neither in the context nor in the predicted event; *hierarchical* models induce a latent context of trees compatible with the input; *sequential* models either induce no latent context at all, or induce a latent sequence of POS tags compatible with the input. Table 1 summarizes the syntactic models and various formulations of surprisal used in this work.

Following Frank and Bod (2011), we consider one type of hierarchical model (PSG's) and two types of sequential models (Markov models and ESN's).

3.1 Phrase-Structure Grammars

PSG's consists of rules expanding a parent node into children nodes in the syntactic tree, with associated probabilities. Frank and Bod (2011) use PSG's that generate POS tag sequences, not words. Under such grammars, the prefix probability of a tag sequence t is the sum of the probabilities of all trees $T : yield(T) = t_1...t_i$, where the probability of each tree T is the product of the probabilities of the rules used in the derivation of T.

Vanilla PCFG's, a special case of PSG's in which the probability of a rule depends only on the identity of the parent node, achieve sub-optimal parsing accuracy relative to grammars in which the probability of each rule depends on a richer context (Charniak, 1996; Johnson, 1998; Klein and Manning, 2003). To this end, Frank and Bod (2011) explore several variants of PSG's conditioned on successively richer contexts, including ancestor models (which condition rule expansions on ancestor nodes from 1-4 levels up in the tree) and ancestor+sibling models (which condition rule expansions on the ancestor's left sibling as well). Both sets of grammars also con-

Authors	Model	Surprisal	Observed Context	Latent Context	Predicted Event
Boston et al. (2008) Demberg and Keller (2008) Roark et al. (2009) Frank and Bod (2011) This Work	Hier.	POS	$t_i....t_{i-1}$	Trees T with yield $t_1...t_{i-1}$	t_i
Demberg and Keller (2008) Roark et al. (2009) This Work	Hier.	Total	$w_1...w_{i-1}$	Trees T with yield $t_1...t_{i-1}$	w_i
Roark et al. (2009) This Work	Hier.	Syntactic-Only	$w_1...w_{i-1}$	Trees T with yield $w_1...w_{i-1}$	t_i
Roark et al. (2009) This Work	Hier.	Lexical-Only	$w_1...w_{i-1}$	Trees T with yield $w_1...w_{i-1}$; t_i	w_i
Frank and Bod (2011) This Work	Seq.	POS	$t_i....t_{i-1}$	–	t_i
–	Seq.	Total	$w_1...w_{i-1}$	$t_1...t_{i-1}$ with yield $w_1...w_{i-1}$	w_i

Table 1: Contexts and events used to produce surprisal measures under various probabilistic syntactic models. T refers to trees; t refers to POS tags; and w refers to words.

dition rule expansions on the current head node[2].

In addition to the grammars over POS tag sequences used by Frank and Bod (2011), we evaluate PSG's over word sequences. We also include the state-of-the-art Berkeley grammar (Petrov and Klein, 2007) in our comparison. Syntactic categories in the Berkeley grammar are automatically split into fine-grained subcategories to improve the likelihood of the training corpus under the model. This increased expressivity allows the parser to achieve state-of-the-art automatic parsing accuracy, but increases grammar size considerably.[3]

3.2 Markov Models

Frank and Bod (2011) use Markov models over POS tag sequences, where the prefix probability of a sequence t is $\prod_i pr(t_i|t_{i-n+1}, t_{i-n+2}...t_{i-1})$. They use three types of smoothing: additive, Good-Turing, and Witten-Bell, and explore values of n from 1 to 3.

[2]or rightmost child node, if the head node is not yet available(Roark, 2001).

[3]To make parsing with the Berkeley grammar tractable under the prefix probability parser, we prune away all rules with probability less than 10^{-4}.

3.3 Echo State Networks

Unlike Markov models, ESN's (Jäger, 2001) can capture long-distance dependencies. ESN's are a type of recurrent neural network (Elman, 1991) in which only the weights from the hidden layer to the output layer are trained; the weights from the input layer to the hidden layer and from the hidden layer to itself are set randomly and do not change. In recurrent networks, the activation of the hidden layer at tag t_i depends not only on the activation of the input layer at tag t_i, but also on the activation of the hidden layer at tag t_{i-1}, which in turn depends on the activation of the hidden layer at tag t_{i-2}, and so forth. The activation of the output layer at tag t_i is therefore a function of all previous input symbols $t_1...t_{i-1}$ in the sequence. The prefix probability of a sequence t under this model is $\prod_i pr(t_i|t_1...t_{i-1})$, where $pr(t_i|t_1...t_{i-1})$ is the normalized activation of the output layer at tag t_i. Frank and Bod (2011) evaluate ESN's with 100, 200...600 hidden nodes.

4 Methods

We use two incremental parsers to calculate surprisals under the hierarchical models. For the PSG's available under the Roark et al. (2009) parser, we use that parser to calculate approximate prefix probabilities using beam search. For the Berkeley grammar, we use a probabilistic Earley parser modified by Levy[4] to calculate exact prefix probabilities using the algorithm of Stolcke (1995). We evaluate each hierarchical model under each type of surprisal (POS, total, lexical-only, and syntactic-only), where possible.

4.1 Data Sets

Each syntactic model is trained on sections 2-21 of the Wall Street Journal (WSJ) portion of the Penn Treebank (Marcus et al., 1994), and tested on the Dundee Corpus (Kennedy and Pynte, 2005), which contains reading time measures for 10 subjects over a corpus of 2,391 sentences of naturally occurring text. Gold-standard POS tags for the Dundee corpus are obtained automatically using the Brill tagger (Brill, 1995).

Frank and Bod (2011) exclude subject/word pairs from evaluation if any of the following conditions hold true: "the word was not fixated, was presented as the first or last on a line, was attached to punctuation, contained more than one capital letter, or contained a non-letter (this included clitics)". This leaves 191,380 subject/word pairs in the data set published by Frank and Bod (2011). Because we consider lexicalized hierarchical models in addition to unlexicalized ones, we additionally exclude subject/word pairs where the word is "unknown" to the model.[5] This leaves us with a total of 148,829 subject/word pairs; all of our reported results refer to this data set.

4.2 Evaluation

Following Frank and Bod (2011), we compare the per-word surprisal predictions from hierarchical and sequential models of syntactic structure along two axes: linguistic accuracy (how well the model explains the test corpus) and psychological accuracy (how well the model explains observed reading times on the test corpus).

[4]The prefix parser is available at: www.http://idiom.ucsd.edu/ rlevy/prefixprobabilityparser.html

[5]We consider words appearing fewer than 5 times in the training data to be unknown.

4.2.1 Linguistic Accuracy

Each model provides surprisal estimates $surprisal(w_i)$. The linguistic accuracy over the test corpus is $\frac{1}{n}\sum_{i=1}^{n} surprisal(w_i)$, where n is the number of words in the test corpus.

4.2.2 Psychological Accuracy

We add each model's per-word surprisal predictions to a linear mixed-effects model of first-pass reading times, then measure the improvement in reading time predictions (according to the deviance information criterion) relative to a baseline model; the resulting decrease in deviance is the psychological accuracy of the language model. Using the `lmer` package for linear mixed-effects models in R (Baayen et al., 2008), we first fit a baseline model to first-pass readings times over the test corpus. Each baseline model contains the following control predictors for each subject/word pair: `sentpos` (position of the word in the sentence), `nrchar` (number of characters in the word), `prevnonfix` (whether the previous word was fixated by the subject), `nextnonfix` (whether the next word was fixated by the subject), `logwordprob` ($log(pr(w_i))$), `logforwprob` ($log(pr(w_i|w_{i-1}))$), and `logbackprob` ($log(pr(w_i|w_{i+1}))$). When fitting each baseline model, we include all control predictors; all significant two-way interactions between them ($|t| \geq 1.96$); by-subject and by-word intercepts; and a by-subject random slope for the predictor that shows the most significant effect (`nrchar`).[6]

We evaluate the statistical significance of the difference in psychological accuracy between two predictors using a nested model comparison. If the model containing both predictors performs significantly better than the model containing only the first predictor under a χ^2 test ($p \leq 0.05$), then the second predictor accounts for variance in reading times above and beyond the first predictor, and vice versa.

[6]In accordance with the methods of Frank and Bod (2011), "Surprisal was not included as a by-subject random slope because of the possibility that participants' sensitivity to surprisal varies more strongly for some sets of surprisal estimates than for others, making the comparisons between language models unreliable. Since subject variability is not currently of interest, it is safer to leave out random surprisal effects."

5 Results

We first replicate the results of Frank and Bod (2011) by obtaining POS surprisal values directly from the authors' published dataset for each syntactic model, then evaluating the psychological accuracy of each of those models relative to the baseline model defined above.[7]

Baseline Model with Additional Lexical N-grams Next, we explore the impact of the lexical n-gram probabilities used as control predictors upon psychological accuracy. Frank and Bod (2011) state that they compute lexical unigram and bigram probabilities via linear interpolation between estimates from the British National Corpus and the Dundee corpus itself (p.c.); upon inspection, we find that the bigram probabilities released in their published data set (which are consistent with their published experimental results) more closely resemble probabilities estimated from the Dundee corpus alone. Because of the small size of the Dundee corpus, lexical bigrams from this corpus alone are unlikely to be representative of a human's language experience.

We augment the lexical bigram probabilities used in the baseline model of Frank and Bod (2011) with additional lexical unigram and bigrams estimated using the SRILM toolkit (Stolcke, 2002) with Kneser-Ney smoothing from three corpora: sections 2-21 of the WSJ portion of the Penn Treebank, the Brown corpus, and the British National corpus. We include these additional predictors and all two-way interactions between them in the baseline model. Figure 1 shows that the relative differences in psychological accuracy between unlexicalized hierarchical and sequential models vanish under this stronger baseline condition.[8]

Unlexicalized Hierarchical Models We then calculate POS surprisal values under each of the ancestor (a1-a4) and the ancestor+sibling (s1-s4) hierarchical models ourselves, using the parser of Roark et al. (2009). We also calculate POS surprisal under the Berkeley grammar (b) using the Levy prefix probability parser. Figure 2 shows the accuracies of these models.[9]

Lexicalized Hierarchical Models Next, we lexicalize the hierarchical models. Figure 3 shows the results of computing total surprisal under each lexicalized hierarchical model (a1-a4T, s1-s4T, and bT). The lexicalized models improve significantly upon their unlexicalized counterparts ($\chi^2 = 7.52 \text{ to } 12.47, p \leq 0.01$) in all cases; by contrast, the unlexicalized models improve significantly upon their lexicalized counterparts ($\chi^2 = 4.05 \text{ to } 5.92, p \leq 0.05$) only in some cases (s1-s4). Each lexicalized model improves significantly upon e4, the best unlexicalized model of Frank and Bod (2011) ($\chi^2 = 6.96 \text{ to } 23.45, p \leq 0.01$), though e4 also achieves a smaller but still significant improvement upon each of the lexicalized models ($\chi^2 = 4.49 \text{ to } 7.58,\ p \leq 0.05$). The lexicalized Berkeley grammar (bT) achieves the highest linguistic and psychological accuracy; the improvement of bT upon e4 is substantial and significant ($\chi^2(1) = 23.45,\ p \leq 0.001$), while the improvement of e4 upon bT is small but still significant ($\chi^2(1) = 4.50,\ p \leq 0.1$). Estimated coefficients for surprisal estimates under each lexicalized hierarchical model are shown in Table 2.[10]

Decomposing Total Surprisal Figure 3 shows the results of decomposing total surprisal (a1-a4T, s1-s4T) into its lexical and syntactic components, then entering both components as predictors into the mixed-effects model (a1-a4LS, s1-s4LS).[11] For each grammar, the psychological accuracy of the surprisal estimates is slightly higher when both lexical and syntactic surprisal are entered as predictors, though the differences are not statistically significant.

[7]The only difference between our results and the original results in Figure 2 of Frank and Bod (2011) is that we evaluate accuracy over a subset of the subject/items pairs used in Frank and Bod (2011) (see Section 4.1 for details).

[8]The psychological accuracies of the best sequential model (e4) and the best hierarchical model (s3) used in Frank and Bod (2011) relative to the stronger baseline with additional lexical n-grams are not significantly different, according to a χ^2 test.

[9]Our POS surprisal estimates have slightly worse linguistic accuracy but slightly better psychological accuracy than Frank and Bod (2011); these differences are likely due to differences in beam settings and in the subset of the WSJ used as training data.

[10]Each surprisal estimate predicts reading times in the expected (positive) direction.

[11]Decomposing surprisal into its lexical and syntactic components is possible with the Levy prefix probability parser as well, but requires modifications to the parser; the Roark et al. (2009) parser computes these quantities explicitly by default.

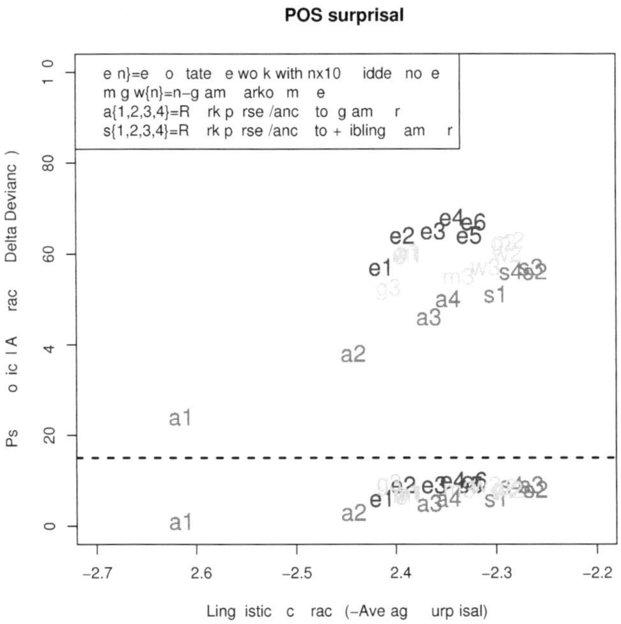

Figure 1: Psychological vs. linguistic accuracy of POS surprisal estimates from unlexicalized sequential and hierarchical models of Frank and Bod (2011) relative to baseline system of Frank and Bod (2011) (shown above dotted line), and relative to a baseline system including additional lexical unigrams and bigrams (shown below dotted line). Incorporating additional lexical n-grams into baseline system virtually eliminates all differences in psychological accuracy among models.

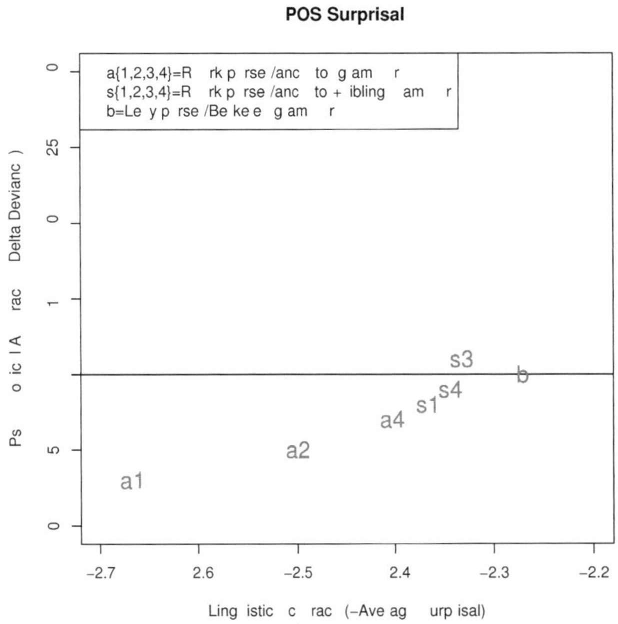

Figure 2: Psychological vs. linguistic accuracy of POS surprisal estimates from unlexicalized hierarchical models used in this work, relative to a baseline system with additional lexical unigrams and bigrams. Horizontal line indicates most psychologically accurate model of Frank and Bod (2011) for ease of comparison.

POS vs. Syntactic-only Surprisal Figures 2 and 4 show the results of computing POS surprisal (a1-a4, s1-s4) and syntactic-only surprisal (a1-a4S, s1-s4S), respectively, under each of the Roark grammars. While syntactic surprisal achieves slightly higher psychological accuracy than POS surprisal for each model, the difference is statistically significant in only one case (s1).

6 Discussion

In the presence of additional lexical n-gram control predictors, all gaps in performance between the unlexicalized sequential and hierarchical models used in Frank and Bod (2011) vanish (Figure 1). Frank and Bod (2011) do not include lexicalized hierarchical models in their study; our results indicate that lexicalizing hierarchical models improves their psychological accuracy significantly compared to the unlexicalized versions. Overall, the lexicalized hierarchical model with the highest linguistic accuracy (Berkeley) also achieves the highest psychological accuracy.

Decomposing total surprisal into its lexical- and syntactic-only components improves psychological accuracy, but this improvement is not statistically significant. Computing syntactic-only surprisal instead of POS surprisal improves psychological accuracy, but this improvement is statistically significant in only one case (s1).

7 Conclusion and Future Work

Frank and Bod (2011) claim that sequential unlexicalized syntactic models predict reading times better than hierarchical unlexicalized syntactic models, and conclude that the human parser is insensitive to hierarchical syntactic structure. We find that the picture is more complicated than this. We show, first, that the gap in psychological accuracy between the unlexicalized hierarchical and sequential models of Frank and Bod (2011) vanishes when additional,

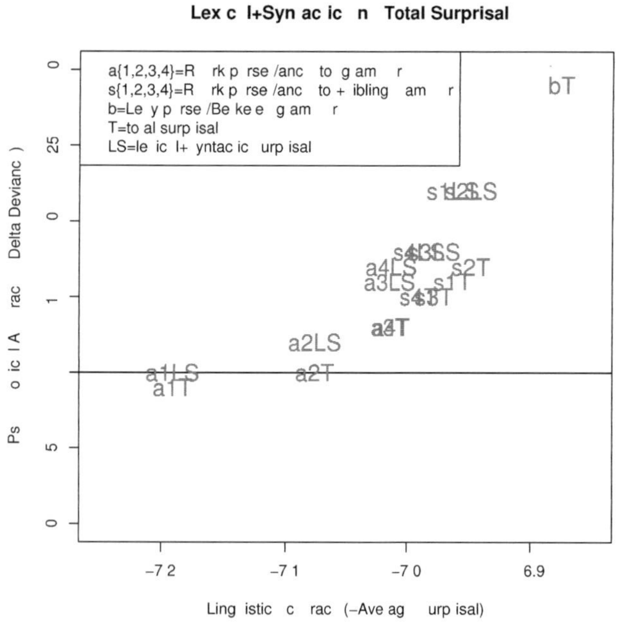

Figure 3: Psychological vs. linguistic accuracy of lexical+syntactic (LS) and total (T) surprisal estimates from lexicalized hierarchical models used in this work, relative to baseline system with additional lexical unigrams and bigrams as control predictors. Decomposing total surprisal into lexical-only and syntactic-components improves psychological accuracy. Horizontal line indicates most psychologically accurate model of (Frank and Bod, 2011).

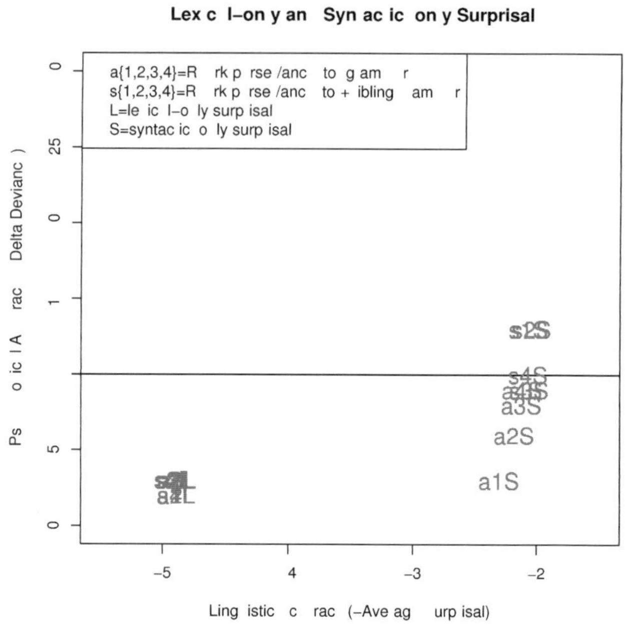

Figure 4: Psychological vs. linguistic accuracy of lexical-only (L) and syntactic-only (S) surprisal estimates from lexicalized hierarchical models used in this work, relative to baseline system with additional lexical unigrams and bigrams as control predictors. On its own, syntactic-only surprisal predicts reading times better than lexical-only surprisal. Horizontal line indicates most psychologically accurate model of (Frank and Bod, 2011).

Surprisal	Coef.	$\|t\|$	Surprisal	Coef.	$\|t\|$
a1LS	0.82	2.61	a1T	1.30	2.98
a2LS	1.01	3.24	a2T	1.38	3.19
a3LS	1.14	3.65	a3T	1.56	3.60
a4LS	1.17	3.76	a4T	1.56	3.64
s1LS	1.38	4.43	s1T	1.71	4.00
s2LS	1.37	4.44	s2T	1.75	4.16
s3LS	1.20	3.90	s3T	1.64	3.91
s4LS	1.21	3.97	s4T	1.62	3.89
bT	3.15	5.34			

Table 2: Estimated coefficients and $|t|$-values for surprisal estimates shown in Figure 3. Coefficients are estimated by adding each surprisal estimate, one at a time, to the baseline model of reading times used in Figure 3.

robustly estimated lexical n-gram probabilities are incorporated as control predictors into the baseline model of reading times. Next, we show that lexicalizing hierarchical grammars improves psychological accuracy significantly. Finally, we show that using better lexicalized hierarchical models improves psychological accuracy still further. Our results demonstrate that the claim of Frank and Bod (2011) that sequential models predict reading times better than hierarchical models is premature, and that further investigation is required.

In future work, we plan to incorporate lexical information into the sequential syntactic models used in Frank and Bod (2011) so that we can compare the hierarchical lexicalized models described here against sequential lexicalized models.

Acknowledgments

The authors thank Stefan Frank for providing the dataset of Frank and Bod (2011) and a detailed specification of their experimental configuration. This research was supported by NSF grant 0953870, NIH grant 1R01HD065829, and funding from the Army Research Laboratory's Cognition & Neuroergonomics Collaborative Technology Alliance.

References

R. H. Baayen, D. J. Davidson, and D. M. Bates. 2008. Mixed-effects modeling with crossed random effects for subjects and items. In *Journal of Memory and Language, 59, pp. 390-412.*

Marisa Ferrara Boston, John Hale, Reinhold Kliegl, Umesh Patil, and Shravan Vasishth. 2008. Parsing costs as predictors of reading difficulty: An evaluation using the potsdam sentence corpus. In *Journal of Eye Movement Research, 2(1):1, pages 1-12.*

Eric Brill. 1995. Transformation-based error-driven learning and natural language processing: A case study in part-of-speech tagging. *Computational linguistics*, 21(4).

Eugene Charniak. 1996. Tree-bank grammars. In *AAAI*.

Vera Demberg and Frank Keller. 2008. Data from eye-tracking corpora as evidence for theories of syntactic processing complexity. In *Cognition, Volume 109, Issue 2, pages 193-210.*

J.L. Elman. 1991. Distributed representations, simple recurrent networks, and grammatical structure. *Machine Learning*, 7(2).

Stefan Frank and Rens Bod. 2011. Insensitivity of the human sentence-processing system to hierarchical structure. In *Psychological Science*.

Edward Gibson, Timothy Desmet, Daniel Grodner, Duane Watson, and Kara Ko. 2005. Reading relative clauses in english. *Cognitive Linguistics*, 16(2).

John Hale. 2001. A probabilistic earley parser as a psycholinguistic model. In *Proceedings of NAACL*.

Herbert Jäger. 2001. The" echo state" approach to analysing and training recurrent neural networks. In *Technical Report GMD 148, German National Research Center for Information Technology*.

Mark Johnson. 1998. Pcfg models of linguistic tree representations. *Computational Linguistics*, 24.

A. Kennedy and J. Pynte. 2005. Parafoveal-on-foveal effects in normal reading. *Vision research*, 45(2).

Jonathan King and Marcel Just. 1991. Individual differences in syntactic processing: The role of working memory. *Journal of memory and language*, 30(5).

Dan Klein and Chris Manning. 2003. Accurate unlexicalized parsing. In *Proceedings of ACL*.

Lars Konieczny and Philipp Döring. 2003. Anticipation of clause-final heads: Evidence from eye-tracking and srns. In *Proceedings of ICCS/ASCS*.

Lars Konieczny. 2000. Locality and parsing complexity. *Journal of Psycholinguistic Research*, 29(6).

E. Lau, C. Stroud, S. Plesch, and C. Phillips. 2006. The role of structural prediction in rapid syntactic analysis. *Brain and Language*, 98(1).

Roger Levy. 2008. Expectation-based syntactic comprehension. *Cognition*.

Mitchell Marcus, Grace Kim, Mary Ann Marcinkiewicz, Robert Macintyre, Ann Bies, Mark Ferguson, Karen Katz, and Britta Schasberger. 1994. The penn treebank: Annotating predicate argument structure,. In *Proceedings of ARPA Human Language Technology Workshop*.

Kentaro Nakatani and Edward Gibson. 2008. Distinguishing theories of syntactic expectation cost in sentence comprehension: Evidence from japanese. *Linguistics*, 46(1).

Joakim Nivre. 2006. *Inductive dependency parsing*, volume 34. Springer Verlag.

Slav Petrov and Dan Klein. 2007. Improved inference for unlexicalized parsing. In *Proceedinngs of HLT-NAACL*.

Brian Roark, Asaf Bachrach, Carlos Cardenas, and Christophe Pallier. 2009. Deriving lexical and syntactic expectation-based measures for psycholinguistic modeling via incremental top-down parsing. In *Proceedings of EMNLP*.

Brian Roark. 2001. Probabilistic top-down parsing and language modeling. *Computational linguistics*, 27(2).

A. Staub and C. Clifton. 2006. Syntactic prediction in language comprehension: Evidence from either... or. *Journal of Experimental Psychology: Learning, Memory, and Cognition*, 32(2).

A. Staub, C. Clifton, and L. Frazier. 2006. Heavy np shift is the parsers last resort: Evidence from eye movements. *Journal of memory and language*, 54(3).

Andreas Stolcke. 1995. An efficient probabilistic context-free parsing algorithm that computes prefix probabilities. *Computational Linguistics*, 21(2).

A. Stolcke. 2002. Srilm-an extensible language modeling toolkit. In *Seventh International Conference on Spoken Language Processing*.

P. Sturt, F. Keller, and A. Dubey. 2010. Syntactic priming in comprehension: Parallelism effects with and without coordination. *Journal of Memory and Language*, 62(4).

Shravan Vasishth and Richard Lewis. 2006. Argument-head distance and processing complexity: Explaining both locality and antilocality effects. *Linguistic Society of America*, 82(4).

Modeling covert event retrieval in logical metonymy: probabilistic and distributional accounts

Alessandra Zarcone, Jason Utt
Institut für Maschinelle Sprachverarbeitung
Universität Stuttgart
{zarconaa,uttjn}@ims.uni-stuttgart.de

Sebastian Padó
Institut für Computerlinguistik
Universität Heidelberg
pado@cl.uni-heidelberg.de

Abstract

Logical metonymies (*The student finished the beer*) represent a challenge to compositionality since they involve semantic content not overtly realized in the sentence (covert events → drinking the beer). We present a contrastive study of two classes of computational models for logical metonymy in German, namely a probabilistic and a distributional, similarity-based model. These are built using the SDEWAC corpus and evaluated against a dataset from a self-paced reading and a probe recognition study for their sensitivity to thematic fit effects via their accuracy in predicting the correct covert event in a metonymical context. The similarity-based models allow for better coverage while maintaining the accuracy of the probabilistic models.

1 Introduction

Logical metonymies (*The student finished the beer*) require the interpretation of a *covert event* which is not overtly realized in the sentence (→ drinking the beer). Logical metonymy has received much attention as it raises issues that are relevant to both theoretical as well as cognitive accounts of language.

On the theoretical side, logical metonymies constitute a challenge for theories of compositionality (Partee et al., 1993; Baggio et al., in press) since their interpretation requires additional, inferred information. There are two main accounts of logical metonymy: According to the *lexical* account, a type clash between an event-subcategorizing verb (*finish*) and an entity-denoting object (*beer*) triggers the recovery of a covert event from complex lexical entries, such as qualia structures (Pustejovsky, 1995). The *pragmatic* account of logical metonymy suggests that covert events are retrieved through post-lexical inferences triggered by our world knowledge and communication principles (Fodor and Lepore, 1998; Cartson, 2002; De Almeida and Dwivedi, 2008).

On the experimental side, logical metonymy leads to higher processing costs (Pylkkänen and McElree, 2006; Baggio et al., 2010). As to covert event retrieval, it has been found that verbs cue fillers with a high thematic fit for their argument positions (e.g. $arrest \xrightarrow{agent} cop$, (Ferretti et al., 2001)) and that verbs and arguments combined cue fillers with a high thematic fit for the remaining argument slots (e.g. $\langle journalist, check\rangle \xrightarrow{patient} spelling$ but $\langle mechanic, check\rangle \xrightarrow{patient} car$ (Bicknell et al., 2010). The interpretation of logical metonymy is also highly sensitive to context (e.g. $\langle confectioner, begin, icing\rangle \xrightarrow{covertevent} spread$ but $\langle child, begin, icing\rangle \xrightarrow{covertevent} eat$ (Zarcone and Padó, 2011; Zarcone et al., 2012). It thus provides an excellent test bed for cognitively plausible computational models of language processing.

We evaluate two classes of computational models for logical metonymy. The classes represent the two main current approaches in lexical semantics: *probabilistic* and *distributional* models. Probabilistic models view the interpretation as the assignment of values to random variables. Their advantage is that they provide a straightforward way to include context, by simply including additional random variables. However, practical estimation of complex models typically involves independence assumptions, which may or may not be appropriate, and such models only take first-order co-occurrence into account[1]. In contrast, distributional models represent linguistic entities as co-occurrence vectors and phrase interpretation as a vector similarity maximization problem. Distributional models typically do not require any independence assumptions, and include second-order co-occurrences. At the same time, how to integrate context into the vector computation is essentially an open research question (Mitchell and Lapata, 2010).

In this paper, we provide the first (to our knowledge) distributional model of logical metonymy by extending the context update of Lenci's ECU model (Lenci, 2011). We compare this model to a previous probabilistic approach (Lapata and Lascarides, 2003a; Lapata et al., 2003b). In contrast to most experimental studies on logical metonymy, which deal with English data (with the exception of Lapata et al. (2003b)), we focus on German. We estimate our models on a large web corpus and evaluate them on a psycholinguistic dataset (Zarcone and Padó, 2011; Zarcone et al., 2012). The task we use to evaluate our models is to distinguish covert events with a high typicality / thematic fit (e.g. *The student finished the beer* $\longrightarrow$ drinking) from low typicality / thematic fit covert events ($\longrightarrow$ *brewing*).

2 Probabilistic models of logical metonymy

Lapata et al. (2003b; 2003a) model the interpretation of a logical metonymy (e.g. *The student finished the beer*) as the joint distribution $P(s,v,o,e)$ of the variables s (the subject, e.g. *student*), v (the metonymic verb, e.g. *finish*), o (the object, e.g. *beer*), e (the covert event, *drinking*).

This model requires independence assumptions for estimation. We present two models with different independence assumptions.

[1]This statement refers to the simple probabilistic models we consider, which are estimated directly from corpus co-occurrence frequencies. The situation is different for more complex probabilistic models, for example generative models that introduce latent variables, which can amount to clustering based on higher-order co-occurrences, as in, e.g., Prescher et al. (2000).

2.1 The SOV_p model

Lapata et al. develop a model which we will refer to as the *SOV_p model*.[2] It assumes a generative process which first generates the covert event e and then generates all other variables based on the choice of e:

$$P(s,v,o,e) \approx P(e)\, P(o|e)\, P(v|e)\, P(s|e)$$

They predict that the selected covert event $\hat{e}$ for a given context is the event which maximizes $P(s,v,o,e)$:

$$\hat{e} = \arg\max_e P(e)\, P(o|e)\, P(v|e)\, P(s|e)$$

These distributions are estimated as follows:

$$\hat{P}(e) = \frac{f(e)}{N}, \quad \hat{P}(o|e) = \frac{f(e \stackrel{o}{\leftarrow} o)}{f(e \stackrel{o}{\leftarrow} \cdot)},$$
$$\hat{P}(v|e) = \frac{f(v \stackrel{c}{\leftarrow} e)}{f(\cdot \stackrel{c}{\leftarrow} e)}, \quad \hat{P}(s|e) = \frac{f(e \stackrel{s}{\leftarrow} s)}{f(e \stackrel{s}{\leftarrow} \cdot)},$$

where N is the number of occurrences of full verbs in the corpus; $f(e)$ is the frequency of the verb e; $f(e \stackrel{o}{\leftarrow} \cdot)$ and $f(e \stackrel{s}{\leftarrow} \cdot)$ are the frequencies of e with a direct object and subject, respectively; and $f(e \stackrel{c}{\leftarrow} \cdot)$ is number of times e is the complement of another full verb.

2.2 The SO_p model

In Lapata et al.'s covert event model, v, the metonymic verb, was used to prime different choices of e for the same object (*begin book*$\longrightarrow$ writing; *enjoy book*$\longrightarrow$ reading). In our dataset (Sec. 4), we keep v constant and consider e only as a function of s and o. Thus, the second model we consider is the *SO_p model* which does not consider v:

$$P(s,v,o,e) \approx P(s,o,e) \approx P(e)\, P(o|e)\, P(s|e)$$

Again, the preferred interpretation $\hat{e}$ is the one that maximizes $P(s,v,o,e)$:

$$\hat{e} = \arg\max_e P(e)\, P(o|e)\, P(s|e)$$

[2]In Lapata et al. (2003b; 2003a), this model is called the *simplified* model to distinguish it from a *full* model. Since the full model performs worse, we do not include it into consideration and use a more neutral name for the simplified model.

3 Similarity-based models

3.1 Distributional semantics

Distributional or vector space semantics (Turney and Pantel, 2010) is a framework for representing word meaning. It builds on the Distributional Hypothesis (Harris, 1954; Miller and Charles, 1991) which states that words occurring in similar contexts are semantically similar. In distributional models, the meaning of a word is represented as a vector whose dimensions represent features of its linguistic context. These features can be chosen in different ways; popular choices are simple words (Schütze, 1992) or lexicalized dependency relations (Lin, 1998; Padó and Lapata, 2007). Semantic similarity can then be approximated by vector similarity using a wide range of similarity metrics (Lee, 1999).

3.1.1 Distributional Memory

A recent multi-purpose framework in distributional semantics is Distributional Memory (DM, Baroni and Lenci (2010)). DM does not immediately construct vectors for words. Instead, it extracts a three-dimensional tensor of weighted *word-link-word* tuples each of which is mapped onto a score by a function σ: $\langle w_1\ l\ w_2 \rangle \rightarrow \mathbb{R}^+$. For example, $\langle$*pencil obj use*$\rangle$ has a higher weight than $\langle$*elephant obj use*$\rangle$. The set of links can be defined in different ways, yielding various DM instances. Baroni and Lenci present DepDM (mainly syntactic links such as $subj\_tr$), LexDM (strongly lexicalized links, e.g., $such\_as$), or TypeDM (syntactic and lexicalized links).[3]

The benefit of the tensor-based representation is that it is general, being applicable to many tasks. Once a task is selected, a dedicated semantic space for this task can be generated efficiently from the tensor. For example, the *word by link-word* space ($W_1 \times LW_2$) contains vectors for the words w_1 whose dimensions are labeled with $\langle l, w_2 \rangle$ pairs. The *word-word by link* space ($W_1W_2 \times L$) contains co-occurrence vectors for word pairs $\langle w_1, w_2 \rangle$ whose dimensions are labeled with l.

3.2 Compositional Distributional Semantics

Probabilistic models can account for compositionality by estimating conditional probabilities. Compositionality is less straightforward in a similarity-based distributional model, because similarity-based distributional models traditionally model meaning at word level. Nevertheless, the last years have seen a wave of distributional models which make progress at building compositional representations of higher-level structures such as noun-adjective or verb-argument combinations (Mitchell and Lapata, 2010; Guevara, 2011; Reddy et al., 2011).

3.2.1 Expectation Composition and Update

Lenci (2011) presents a model to predict the degree of thematic fit for verb-argument combinations: the Expectation Composition and Update (ECU) model. More specifically, the goal of ECU is explain how the choice of a specific subject for a given verb impacts the semantic expectation for possible objects. For example, the verb *draw* alone might have fair, but not very high, expectations for the two possible objects *landscape* and *card*. When it is combined with the subject *painter*, the resulting phrase *painter draw* the expectation for the object *landscape* should increase, while it should drop for *card*.

The idea behind ECU is to first compute the verb's own expectations for the object from a TypeDM $W_1 \times LW_2$ matrix and then update it with the subject's expectations for the object, as mediated by the TypeDM *verb* link type.[4] More formally, the verb's expectations for the object are defined as

$$EX_V(v) = \lambda o.\, \sigma(\langle v\ obj^{-1}\ o \rangle)$$

The subject's expectations for the object are

$$EX_S(s) = \lambda o.\, \sigma(\langle s\ verb\ o \rangle)$$

And the updated expectation is

$$EX_{SV}(s, v) = \lambda o.\, EX_V(v)(o) \circ EX_S(s)(o)$$

where $\circ$ is a composition operation which Lenci instantiates as sum and product, following common practice in compositional distributional semantics (Mitchell and Lapata, 2010). The product composition approximates a conjunction, promoting objects that are strongly preferred by both verb and subject. It is, however, also prone to sparsity problems as well

[3] l^{-1} is used to denote the inverse link of l (i.e., exchanging the positions of w_1 and w_2).

[4] In DM, *verb* directly connects the subject and the object of transitive verb instances, e.g $\langle$*marine verb gun*$\rangle$.

shortcomings of the scoring function σ. The sum composition is more akin to a disjunction where it suffices that an object is strongly preferred by either the verb or the subject.

It would be possible to use these scores as direct estimates of expectations, however, since EX_{SV} contains three lexical variables, sparsity is a major issue. ECU thus introduces a distributional generalization step. It only uses the updated expectations to identify the 20 most expected nouns for the object position. It then determines the prototype of the updated expectations as the centroid of their $W_1 \times LW_2$ vectors. Now, the thematic fit for any noun can be computed as the similarity of its vector to the prototype.

Lenci evaluates ECU against a dataset from Bicknell et al. (2010), where objects (e.g. *spelling*) are matched with a high-typicality subject-verb combinations (e.g. ⟨*journalist, check*⟩ - high thematic fit) and with a low-typicality subject-verb combination (e.g. ⟨*mechanic, check*⟩ - low thematic fit). ECU is in fact able to correctly distinguish between the two contexts differing in thematic fit with the object.

3.3 Cognitive relevance

Similarity-based models build upon the Distributional Hypothesis, which, in its strong version, is a cognitive hypothesis about the form of semantic representations (Lenci, 2008): the distributional behavior of a word reflects its semantic behavior but is also a direct correlate of its semantic content at the cognitive level. Also, similarity-based models are highly compatible with known features of human cognition, such as graded category membership (Rosch, 1975) or multiple sense activation (Erk, 2010). Their cognitive relevance for language has been supported by studies of child lexical development (Li et al., 2004), category-related deficits (Vigliocco et al., 2004), selectional preferences (Erk, 2007), event types (Zarcone and Lenci, 2008) and more (see Landauer et al. (2007) and Baroni and Lenci (2010) for a review).

3.4 Modeling Logical Metonymy with ECU

3.4.1 Logical Metonymy as Thematic Fit

The hypothesis that we follow in this paper is that the ECU model can also be used, with modifications, to predict the interpretation of logical metonymy. The underlying assumption is that the interpretation of logical metonymy is essentially the recovery of a covert event with a maximal thematic fit (high-typicality) and can thus make use of ECU's mechanisms to treat verb-argument composition. Strong evidence for this assumption has been found in psycholinguistic studies, which have established that thematic fit dynamically affects processing, with on-line updates of expectations for typical fillers during the incremental processing of linguistic input (see McRae and Matsuki (2009) for a review). Thus, we can hope to transfer the benefits of similarity-based models (notably, high coverage) to the interpretation of logical metonymy.

3.4.2 Extending ECU

The ECU model nevertheless requires some modifications to be applicable to logical metonymy. Both the entity of interest and the knowledge sources change. The entity of interest used to be the object of the sentence; now it is the covert event, which we will denote with e. As for knowledge sources, there are three sources in logical metonymy. These are (a), the subject (compare *the author began the beer* and *the reader began the book*)); (b), the object *the reader began the book* vs. *the reader began the sandwich*); and (c), the metonymic verb (compare *Peter began the report* vs. *Peter enjoyed the report*).

The basic equations of ECU can be applied to this new scenario as follows. We first formulate three basic equations that express the expectations of the covert event given the subject, object, and metonymic verb individually. They are all derived from direct dependency relations in the DM tensor (e.g., the novel metonymic verb–covert event relation from the verbal complement relation):

$$EX_S(s) = \lambda e.\, \sigma(\langle s\ \textit{subj}\ e\rangle)$$
$$EX_O(o) = \lambda e.\, \sigma(\langle o\ \textit{obj}\ e\rangle)$$
$$EX_V(v) = \lambda e.\, \sigma(\langle v\ \textit{comp}^{-1}\ e\rangle)$$

To combine (or update) these basic expectations into a final expectation, we propose two variants:

ECU SOV In this model, we compose all three expectations:

$$EX_{SOV}(s,v,o) = \lambda e.\, EX_S(s)(e) \circ EX_O(o)(e) \circ EX_V(v)(e)$$

	CE	
	high thematic fit	low thematic fit
Der *Konditor* begann, die *Glasur* The baker started the icing	**aufzutragen.** **to spread.**	**zu essen.** **to eat.**
Das *Kind* begann, die *Glasur* The child started the icing	**zu essen.** **to eat.**	**aufzutragen.** **to spread.**

Table 1: Example materials for the self-paced reading and probe recognition studies

We will refer to this model as SOV_Σ when the composition function is sum, and as the SOV_Π model when the composition function is product.

ECU SO Analogous to the SO probabilistic model, this model abstracts away from the metonymic verb. We assume most information about an event to be determined by the subject and object:

$$EX_{SO}(n, n') = \lambda e.\, EX_S(n)(e) \circ EX_O(n')(e)$$

After the update, the prototype computation proceeds as defined in the original ECU.

We will refer to this model as SO_Σ when the composition function is sum, and as the SO_Π model when the composition function is product.

4 Experimental Setup

We evaluate the probabilistic models (Sec. 2) and the similarity-based models (Sec. 3) on a dataset constructed from two German psycholinguistic studies on logical metonymy. One study used self-paced reading and the second one probe recognition.

Dataset The dataset we use is composed of 96 sentences. There are 24 sets of four $\langle s, v, o, e\rangle$ tuples, where s is the object, v the metonymic verb, o the object and e the covert event. The materials are illustrated in Table 1. As can be seen, all tuples within a set share the same metonymic verb and the same object. Each of the two subject e is matched once with a high-typicality covert event and once with a low-typicality covert event. This results in 2 high-typicality tuples and 2 low-typicality tuples in each set. Typical events (e) were elicited by 20 participants given the corresponding object o, subjects were elicited by 10 participants as the prototypical agents subjects for each e, o combination.

The experiments yielded a main effect of typicality on self-paced reading times (Zarcone and Padó, 2011) and on probe recognition latencies (Zarcone et al., 2012): typical events involved in logical metonymy interpretation are read faster and take longer to be rejected as probe words after sentences which evoke them. The effect is seen early on (after the patient position in the self-paced reading and at short ISI for the probe recognition), suggesting that knowledge of typical events is quickly integrated in processing and that participants access a broader pool of knowledge than what has traditionally been argued to be in the lexical entries of nouns (Pustejovsky, 1995). The finding is in agreement with results of psycholinguistic studies which challenge the very distinction between world knowledge and linguistic knowledge (Hagoort et al., 2004; McRae and Matsuki, 2009).

DM for German Since DM exists only for English, we constructed a German analog using the 884M word SDEWAC web corpus (Faaß et al., 2010) parsed with the MATE German dependency parser (Bohnet, 2010).

From this corpus, we extract 55M instances of simple syntactic relations (*subj_tr, subj_intr, obj, iobj, comp, nmod*) and 104M instances of lexicalized patterns such as *noun–prep–noun* e.g. ⟨*Recht auf Auskunft*⟩ (⟨*right to information*⟩), or *adj–noun-(of)-noun* such as ⟨*strittig Entscheidung Schiedsrichter*⟩ (⟨*contested decision referee*⟩). These lexicalized patterns make our model roughly similar to the English TypeDM model (Sec. 3.1.1).

As for σ, we used local mutual information (LMI) as proposed by Baroni and Lenci (2010). The LMI of a triple is defined as $O_{w_1 l w_2} \log(O_{w_1 l w_2}/E_{w_1 l w_2})$, where $O_{w_1 l w_2}$ is the observed co-occurrence frequency of the triple and $E_{w_1 l w_2}$ its expected co-occurrence frequency (under the assumption of independence). Like standard MI, LMI measures the informativity or surprisal of a co-occurrence, but weighs it by the observed frequency to avoid the overestimation for low-probability events.

4.1 Task

We evaluate the models using a binary selection task, similar to Lenci (2011). Given a triple $\langle s, v, o\rangle$ and a pair of covert events e, e' (cf. rows in Tab. 1), the task is to pick the high-typicality covert event for the given triple: ⟨*Chauffeur*, *vermeiden*, *Auto*⟩ → *fahren*/*reparieren* (⟨*driver*, *avoid*, *car*⟩ → *drive*/*repair*). Since our dataset consists of 96 sentences, we have 48 such contexts.

With the probabilistic models, we compare the probabilities $P(s, v, o, e)$ and $P(s, v, o, e')$ (ignoring v in the SO model). Analogously, for the similarity-based models, we compute the similarities of the vectors for e and e' to the prototype vectors for the expectations $EX_{SOV}(s, v, o)$ and predict the one with higher similarity. For the simplified ECU SO model, we use $EX_{SO}(s, o)$ as the point of comparison.

4.2 Baseline

Following the baseline choice in Lapata et al. (2003b), we evaluated the probabilistic models against a baseline (B_p) which, given a $\langle s, v, o\rangle$ triplet (e.g. ⟨*Chauffeur, vermeiden, Auto*⟩), scores a "hit" if the $\hat{P}(e|o)$ for the high-typicality e is higher than the $\hat{P}(e|o)$ for the low-typicality e. The similarity-based models were evaluated against a baseline (B_s) which, given an $\langle s, v, o\rangle$ triplet (e.g. ⟨*Chauffeur, vermeiden, Auto*⟩), makes a correct prediction if the prototypical event vector for o has a higher thematic fit (i.e. similarity) with the high-typicality e than with the low-typicality e.

Since our dataset is counterbalanced – that is, each covert event appears once as the high-typicality event for a given object (with a congruent subject) and once as the low-typicality event – the baseline predicts the correct covert event in exactly 50% of the cases. Note, however, that this is not a *random* baseline: the choice of the covert event is made deterministically on the basis of the input parameters.

4.3 Evaluation measures

We evaluate the output of the model with the standard measures coverage and accuracy. *Coverage* is defined as the percentage of datapoints for which a model can make a prediction. Lack of coverage arises primarily from sparsity, that is, zero counts for co-occurrences that are necessary in the estimation of a model. *Accuracy* is computed on the covered contexts only, as the ratio of correct predictions to the number of predictions of the model. This allows us to judge the quality of the model's predictions independent of its coverage.

We also consider a measure that combines coverage and accuracy, *Backoff Accuracy*, defined as: *coverage* × *accuracy* + ((1 − *coverage*) × 0.5). Backoff Accuracy emulates a backoff procedure: the model's predictions are adopted where they are available; for the remaining datapoints, it assumes baseline performance (in the current setup, 50%). The Backoff Accuracy of low-coverage models tends to degrade towards baseline performance.

We determine the significance of differences between models with a χ^2 test, applied to a 2×2 contingency matrix containing the number of correct and incorrect answers. Datapoints outside a model's coverage count half for each category, which corresponds exactly to the definition of Backoff Accuracy.

5 Results

The results are shown in Table 2. Looking at the probabilistic models, we find SO_p yields better coverage and better accuracy than SOV_p (Lapata's *simplified model*). It is worth noting the large difference in coverage, namely .75 as opposed to .44: The SOV_p model is unable to make a prediction for more than half of all contexts. This is due to the fact that many $\langle o, v\rangle$ combinations are unattested in the corpus. Even on those contexts for which the probabilistic SOV_p model can make a prediction, it is less reliable than the more general SO_p model (0.62 versus 0.75 accuracy). This indicates that, at least on our dataset, the metonymic verb does not systematically help to predict the covert event; it rather harms performance by introducing noisy estimates. As the lower half of the Table shows, the SOV_p model does not significantly outperform any other model (including both baselines B_p and B_s).

The distributional models do not have such coverage issues. The main problematic combination for the similarity model is ⟨*Pizzabote hassen Pizza*⟩ (i.e. ⟨*Pizza delivery man hate pizza*⟩) which is paired with the covert events *liefern (deliver)* and *backen (bake)*. The computation of ECU predictions for

	Probabilistic Models			Similarity-based Models				
	B_p	SOV_p	SO_p	B_s	SOV_Σ	SOV_Π	SO_Σ	SO_Π
Accuracy	0.50	0.62	0.75	0.50	0.68	0.56	0.68	0.70
Coverage	1.00	0.44	0.75	1.00	0.98	0.94	0.98	0.98
Backoff Accuracy	0.50	0.55	**0.69**	0.50	0.68	0.56	0.68	**0.70**

		Probabilistic Models			Similarity-based Models				
		B_p	SOV_p	SO_p	B_s	SOV_Σ	SOV_Π	SO_Σ	SO_Π
Prob.	B_p								
	SOV_p	-							
	SO_p	*	-						
Similarity	B_s	-	-	*					
	SOV_Σ	*	-	-	*				
	SOV_Π	-	-	-	-	-			
	SO_Σ	*	-	-	*	-	-		
	SO_Π	**	$*^\dagger$	-	**	-	$*^\dagger$	-	

Table 2: Results (above) and significance levels for difference in backoff accuracy determined by χ^2-test (below) for all probabilistic and similarity-based models (**: p<0.01, *: p≤0.05, -: p>0.05). For $*^\dagger$ ($SO_\Pi - SOV_p$ and $SO_\Pi - SOV_\Pi$) p was just above 0.05 (p=0.053).

this combination requires corpus transitive corpus constructions for *Pizzabote*, in the corpus it is only attested once as the subject of the intransitive verb *kommen* (*come*).

Among distributional models, the difference between SO and SOV is not as clear-cut as on the probabilistic side. We observe an interaction with the composition operation. Sum is less sensitive to complexity of updating: for sum models, the inclusion of the metonymic verb (SOV_Σ vs. SOV_Π) does not make any difference. On the side of the product models, there is a major difference similar to the one for the probabilistic models: SOV_Π is the worst model at near-baseline performance, and SO_Π is the best one. This supports our interpretation from above that the metonymic model introduces noisy expectations which, in the product model, have the potential of disrupting the update process.

Comparing the best models from the probabilistic and similarity-based classes (SO_p and SO_Π), we find that both significantly outperform the baselines. This shows that the subject contributes to the models with a significant improvement over the baseline models, which are only informed by the object. Their backoff accuracies do not significantly differ from one another, which is not surprising given the small size of our dataset, however, the similarity-based model outperforms the probabilistic model by 1% Backoff Accuracy. The two models have substantially different profiles: the accuracy of the probabilistic model is 5% higher (0.70 vs. 0.75); at the same time, its coverage is much lower. It covers only 75% of the contexts, while the distributional model SO_Π covers all but one (98%).

6 Discussion

As mentioned above, the main issue with the probabilistic models is coverage. This is due to the reliance of these models on first-order co-occurrence.

For example, probabilistic models cannot assign a probability to any of the triples ⟨*Dieb/Juwelier schmuggeln/schleifen Diamant*⟩ (⟨*thief/jeweler smuggle/cut diamond*⟩), since the subjects do not occur with either of the verbs in corpus, even though *Diamant* does occur as the object of both.

In contrast, the similarity-based models are able to compute expectations for these triples from second-order co-occurrences by taking into account other verbs that co-occur with *Diamant*. The ECU model is not punished by the extra context, as both *Dieb* and *Diamant* are associated with the verbs: *stehlen* (steal),

$EX_{SO}(\langle$*Chauffeur, Auto*$\rangle)$		$EX_{SO}(\langle$*Mechaniker, Auto*$\rangle)$	
fahren	*(drive)*	*bauen*	*(build)*
parken	*(park)*	*lassen*	*(let/leave)*
lassen	*(let/leave)*	*besitzen*	*(own)*
geben	*(give)*	*reparieren*	*(repair)*
sehen	*(see)*	*brauchen*	*(need)*
bringen	*(bring)*	*sehen*	*(see)*
steuern	*(steer)*	*benutzen*	*(use)*
halten	*(keep/hold)*	*stellen*	*(put)*

Table 3: Updated expectations in SO_{Π} for *Chauffeur* (*chauffeur*), *Mechaniker* (*mechanic*) and *Auto* (*car*).

rauben (thieve), *holen* (*get*), *entwenden* (*purloin*), *erbeuten* (*snatch*), *verkaufen* (*sell*), *nehmen* (*take*), *klauen* (*swipe*). We also note that these are typical events for a thief, which fits the intuition that *Dieb* is more predictive of the event than *Diamant*.

For both ⟨*Chauffeur Auto*⟩ and ⟨*Mechaniker Auto*⟩ the probabilistic model predicts *fahren* due to the high overall frequency of *fahren*.[5] The distributional model, however, takes the mutual information into account and is thus able to determine events that are more strongly associated with *Mechaniker* (e.g. *bauen, reparieren*, etc.) while at the same time discounting the uninformative verb *fahren*.

There are, however, items that all models have difficulty with. Three such cases are due to a frequency disparity between the high and low-typicality event. E.g. for ⟨*Lehrerin Klausur benoten/schreiben*⟩ (⟨*teacher exam grade/take*⟩), *schreiben* occurs much more frequently than *benoten*. In the case of ⟨*Schüler Geschichte lernen/schreiben*⟩ (⟨*student story learn/write*⟩), none of the models or baselines correctly assigned *lernen*. The probabilistic models are influenced by the very frequent *Geschichte schreiben* which is part of an idiomatic expression (*to write history*). On the other hand, the distributional models judge the *story* and *history* sense of the word to have the most informative events, e.g. *erzählen* (*tell*), *lesen* (*read*), *hören* (*hear*), *erfinden* (*invent*), and *studieren* (*study*), *lehren* (*teach*).

The baselines were able to correctly choose *auspacken* (*unwrap*) over *einpacken* (*wrap*) for ⟨*Geburtstagskind Geschenk*⟩ (⟨*birthday-boy/girl present*⟩) while the models were not. The probabilistic models lacked coverage and were not able to make a prediction. For the distributional models, while both *auspacken* and *verpacken* (*wrap*) are highly associated with *Geschenk*, the most strongly associated actions of *Geburtstagskind* are extraordinarily diverse, e.g.: *bekommen* (*receive*), *sagen* (*say*), *auffuttern* (*eat up*), *herumkommandieren* (*boss around*), *ausblasen* (*blow out*). Neither of the events of interest though were highly associated.

[5] The combination *Mechaniker fahren* was seen once more often than *Mechaniker reparieren*.

7 Future Work

We see a possible improvement in the choice of the number of fillers, with which we construct the prototype vectors. A smaller number might lead to less noisy prototypes.

It has been shown (Bergsma et al., 2010) that the meaning of the prefix verb can be accurately predicted using the stem's vector, when compositionality applies. We suspect covert events that are prefix verbs to suffer from sparser representations than the vectors of their stem. E.g., *absaugen* (*vacuum off*) is much less frequent than the semantically nearly identical *saugen* (*vacuum*). Thus, by leveraging the richer representation of the stem, our distributional models could more likely assign the correct event.

8 Conclusions

We have presented a contrastive study of two classes of computational models, probabilistic and distributional similarity-based ones, for the prediction of covert events for German logical metonymies.

We found that while both model classes models outperform baselines which only take into account information coming from the object, similarity-based models rival and even outperform probabilistic models. The reason is that probabilistic models have to rely on first-order co-occurrence information which suffers from sparsity issues even in large web corpora. This is particularly true for languages like German that have a complex morphology, which tends to aggravate sparsity (e.g., through compound nouns).

In contrast, similarity-based models can take advantage of higher-order co-occurrences. Provided that some care is taken to identify reasonable vector composition strategies, they can maintain the accuracy of probabilistic models while guaranteeing higher coverage.

Acknowledgments

We would like to thank Alessandro Lenci, Siva Reddy and Sabine Schulte im Walde for useful feedback and discussion. The research for this paper has been funded by the German Research Foundation (Deutsche Forschungsgemeinschaft) as part of the SFB 732 "Incremental specification in context" / project D6 "Lexical-semantic factors in event interpretation" at the University of Stuttgart.

References

Giosuè Baggio, Travis Chroma, Michiel van Lambalgen, and Peter Hagoort. 2010. Coercion and compositionality. *Journal of Cognitive Neuroscience*, 22(9):2131–2140.

Giosuè Baggio, Michiel van Lambalgen, and Peter Hagoort. in press. The processing consequences of compositionality. In *The Oxford Handbook of Compositionality*. Oxford University Press.

Marco Baroni and Alessandro Lenci. 2010. Distributional memory: A general framework for corpus-based semantics. *Computational Linguistics*, 36(4):1–49.

Shane Bergsma, Aditya Bhargava, Hua He, and Grzegorz Kondrak. 2010. Predicting the semantic compositionality of prefix verbs. In *Proceedings of the 2010 Conference on Empirical Methods in Natural Language Processing*, pages 293–303, Cambridge, MA, October. Association for Computational Linguistics.

Klinton Bicknell, Jeffrey L. Elman, Mary Hare, Ken McRae, and Marta Kutas. 2010. Effects of event knowledge in processing verbal arguments. *Journal of Memory and Language*, 63(4):489–505.

Bernd Bohnet. 2010. Top accuracy and fast dependency parsing is not a contradiction. In *Proceedings of the 23rd International Conference on Computational Linguistics*, pages 89–97, Beijing, China.

Robyn Cartson. 2002. *Thoughts and utterances*. Blackwell.

Roberto G. De Almeida and Veena D. Dwivedi. 2008. Coercion without lexical decomposition: Type-shifting effects revisited. *Canadian Journal of Linguistics*, 53(2/3):301–326.

Katrin Erk. 2007. A simple, similarity-based model for selectional preferences. In *Proceedings of ACL*, Prague, Czech Republic.

Katrin Erk. 2010. What is word meaning, really? (and how can distributional models help us describe it?). In *Proceedings of the workshop on Geometrical Models of Natural Language Semantics (GEMS)*, Uppsala, Sweden.

Gertrud Faaß, Ulrich Heid, and Helmut Schmid. 2010. Design and Application of a Gold Standard for Morphological Analysis: SMOR as an Example of Morphological Evaluation. In *Proceedings of the Seventh International Conference on Language Resources and Evaluation (LREC'10)*, Valletta, Malta.

T. R. Ferretti, K. McRae, and A. Hatherell. 2001. Integrating verbs, situation schemas and thematic role concept. *Journal of Memory and Language*, 44:516–547.

Jerry A. Fodor and Ernie Lepore. 1998. The emptiness of the lexicon: Reflections on James Pustejovsky's The Generative Lexicon. *Linguistic Inquiry*, 29(2):269–288.

Emiliano Raul Guevara. 2011. Computing semantic compositionality in distributional semantics. In *Proceedings of IWCS-2011*, Oxford, UK.

Peter Hagoort, Lea Hald, Marcel Bastiaansen, and Karl Magnus Petersson. 2004. Integration of word meaning and world knowledge in language comprehension. *Science*, 304:438–441.

Zelig S. Harris. 1954. Distributional structure. *Word*, 10(23):146–162.

Thomas K. Landauer, Danielle S. McNamara, Simon Dennis, and Walter Kintsch, editors. 2007. *Handbook of Latent Semantic Analysis*. Lawrence Erlbaum Associates Publishers, Mahwah, NJ, US.

Mirella Lapata and Alex Lascarides. 2003a. A probabilistic account of logical metonymy. *Computational Linguistics*, 29(2):263–317.

Mirella Lapata, Frank Keller, and Christoph Scheepers. 2003b. Intra-sentential context effects on the interpretation of logical metonymy. *Cognitive Science*, 27(4):649–668.

Lillian Lee. 1999. Measures of Distributional Similarity. In *Proceedings of the 37th annual meeting of the Association for Computational Linguistics on Computational Linguistics*, College Park, MA.

Alessandro Lenci. 2008. Distributional semantics in linguistic and cognitive research. *From context to meaning: Distributional models of the lexicon in linguistics and cognitive science. Special issue of the Italian Journal of Linguistics*, 20(1):1–31.

Alessandro Lenci. 2011. Composing and updating verb argument expectations: A distributional semantic model. In *Proceedings of the 2nd Workshop on Cognitive Modeling and Computational Linguistics*, pages 58–66, Portland, Oregon.

Ping Li, Igor Farkas, and Brian MacWhinney. 2004. Early lexical development in a self-organizing neural network. *Neural Networks*, 17:1345–1362.

Dekang Lin. 1998. Automatic retrieval and clustering of similar words. In *Proceedings of COLING/ACL*, pages 768–774, Montreal, QC.

Ken McRae and Kazunaga Matsuki. 2009. People use their knowledge of common events to understand language, and do so as quickly as possible. *Language and Linguistics Compass*, 3/6:1417–1429.

George A. Miller and Walter G. Charles. 1991. Contextual correlates of semantic similarity. *Language and Cognitive Processes*, 6(1):1–28.

Jeff Mitchell and Mirella Lapata. 2010. Composition in distributional models of semantics. *Cognitive Science*, 34(8):1388–1429.

Sebastian Padó and Mirella Lapata. 2007. Dependency-based construction of semantic space models. *Computational Linguistics*, 33:161–199, June.

Barbara H. Partee, Alice ter Meulen, and Robert E. Wall. 1993. *Mathematical Methods in Linguistics*. Kluwer.

Detlef Prescher, Stefan Riezler, and Mats Rooth. 2000. Using a Probabilistic Class-Based Lexicon for Lexical Ambiguity Resolution. In *Proceedings of COLING 2000*, Saarbrücken, Germany.

James Pustejovsky. 1995. *The Generative Lexicon*. MIT Press.

Liina Pylkkänen and Brian McElree. 2006. The syntax-semantic interface: On-line composition of sentence meaning. In *Handbook of Psycholinguistics*, pages 537–577. Elsevier.

Siva Reddy, Diana McCarthy, and Suresh Manandhar. 2011. An empirical study on compositionality in compound nouns. In *Proceedings of IJCNLP 2011*, Chiang Mai, Thailand.

Eleanor Rosch. 1975. Cognitive representations of semantic categories. *Journal of Experimental Psychology: General*, 104:192–233.

Hinrich Schütze. 1992. Dimensions of meaning. In *Proceedings of Supercomputing '92*, pages 787 –796.

Peter D. Turney and Patrick Pantel. 2010. From frequency to meaning: Vector space models of semantics. *Journal of Artificial Intelligence Research*, 37:141–188.

Gabriella Vigliocco, David P. Vinson, William Lewis, and Merrill F. Garrett. 2004. Representing the meanings of object and action words: The featural and unitary semantic space hypothesis. *Cognitive Psychology*, 48(4):422–488.

Alessandra Zarcone and Alessandro Lenci. 2008. Computational models for event type classification in context. In *Proceedings of the Sixth International Conference on Language Resources and Evaluation (LREC'08)*, Marrakech, Morocco. ELRA.

Alessandra Zarcone and Sebastian Padó. 2011. Generalized event knowledge in logical metonymy resolution. In *Proceedings of the 33rd Annual Conference of the Cognitive Science Society*, pages 944–949, Austin, TX.

Alessandra Zarcone, Sebastian Padó, and Alessandro Lenci. 2012. Inferring covert events in logical metonymies: a probe recognition experiment. In *Proceedings of the 34th Annual Conference of the Cognitive Science Society*, Austin, TX.

A Computational Model of Memory, Attention, and Word Learning

Aida Nematzadeh, Afsaneh Fazly, and Suzanne Stevenson
Department of Computer Science
University of Toronto
{aida,afsaneh,suzanne}@cs.toronto.edu

Abstract

There is considerable evidence that people generally learn items better when the presentation of items is distributed over a period of time (the spacing effect). We hypothesize that both forgetting and attention to novelty play a role in the spacing effect in word learning. We build an incremental probabilistic computational model of word learning that incorporates a forgetting and attentional mechanism. Our model accounts for experimental results on children as well as several patterns observed in adults.

1 Memory, Attention, and Word Learning

Learning the meaning of words is an important component of language acquisition, and an extremely challenging task faced by young children (*e.g.*, Carey, 1978; Bloom, 2000). Much psycholinguistic research has investigated the mechanisms underlying early word learning, and the factors that may facilitate or hinder this process (*e.g.*, Quine, 1960; Markman and Wachtel, 1988; Golinkoff et al., 1992; Carpenter et al., 1998). Computational modeling has been critical in this endeavor, by giving precise accounts of the possible processes and influences involved (*e.g.*, Siskind, 1996; Regier, 2005; Yu, 2005; Fazly et al., 2010). However, computational models of word learning have generally not given sufficient attention to the broader interactions of language acquisition with other aspects of cognition and cognitive development.

Memory limitations and attentional mechanisms are of particular interest, with recent computational studies reconfirming their important role in aspects of word learning. For example, Frank et al. (2010) show that memory limitations are key to matching human performance in a model of word segmentation, while Smith et al. (2010) further demonstrate how attention plays a role in word learning by forming the basis for abstracting over the input. But much potential remains for computational modeling to contribute to a better understanding of the role of memory and attention in word learning.

One area where there is much experimental evidence relevant to these interactions is in the investigation of the *spacing effect* in learning (Ebbinghaus, 1885; Glenberg, 1979; Dempster, 1996; Cepeda et al., 2006). The observation is that people generally show better learning when the presentations of the target items to be learned are "spaced" — i.e., distributed over a period of time — instead of being "massed" — i.e., presented together one after the other. Investigations of the spacing effect often use a word learning task as the target learning event, and such studies have looked at the performance of adults as well as children (Glenberg, 1976; Pavlik and Anderson, 2005; Vlach et al., 2008). While this work involves controlled laboratory conditions, the spacing effect is very robust across domains and tasks (Dempster, 1989), suggesting that the underlying cognitive processes likely play a role in natural conditions of word learning as well.

Hypothesized explanations for the spacing effect have included both memory limitations and attention. For example, many researchers assume that the process of forgetting is responsible for the improved performance in the spaced presentation: Because participants forget more of what they have learned in the longer interval, they learn more from subsequent presentations (Melton, 1967; Jacoby, 1978;

Cuddy and Jacoby, 1982). However, the precise relation between forgetting and improved learning has not been made clear. It has also been proposed that subjects attend more to items in the spaced presentation because accessing less recent (more novel) items in memory requires more effort or attention (Hintzman, 1974). However, the precise attentional mechanism at work in the spacing experiments is not completely understood.

While such proposals have been discussed for many years, to our knowledge, there is as yet no detailed computational model of the precise manner in which forgetting and attention to novelty play a role in the spacing effect. Moreover, while mathematical models of the effect help to clarify its properties (Pavlik and Anderson, 2005), it is very important to situate these general cognitive mechanisms within a model of word learning in order to understand clearly how these various processes might interact in the natural word learning setting.

We address this gap by considering memory constraints and attentional mechanisms in the context of a computational model of word-meaning acquisition. Specifically, we change an existing probabilistic incremental model of word learning (Fazly et al., 2010) by integrating two new factors: (i) a forgetting mechanism that causes the learned associations between words and meanings to decay over time; and (ii) a mechanism that simulates the effects of attention to novelty on in-the-moment learning. The result is a more cognitively plausible word learning model that includes a precise formulation of both forgetting and attention to novelty. In simulations using this new model, we show that a possible explanation for the spacing effect is the interplay of these two mechanisms, neither of which on its own can account for the effect.

2 The Computational Model

We extend the model of Fazly et al. (2010) — henceforth referred to as FAS10 — by integrating new functionality to capture forgetting and attention to novelty. The model of FAS10 is an appropriate starting point for our study because it is an incremental model of word learning that learns probabilistic associations between words and their semantic properties from naturalistic data. Nonetheless, the model assumes equal attention to all words and objects present in the input, and, although incremental, it has a perfect memory for the internal representation of each processed input. Hence, as we will show, it is incapable of simulating the spacing effects observed in humans.

2.1 The FAS10 Model

The input to the model is a sequence of utterances (a set of words), each paired with a scene representation (a set of semantic features, representing what is perceived when the words are heard), as in:

> **Utterance:** { *she, drinks, milk* }
> **Scene:** { ANIMATE, PERSON, FEMALE, CONSUME, DRINK, SUBSTANCE, FOOD, DAIRY-PRODUCT }

For each word, the model of FAS10 learns a probability distribution over all possible features, $p(.|w)$, called the *meaning probability* of the word. Before processing any input, all features are equally likely for a word, and the word's meaning probability is uniform over all features. At each time step t, an input utterance–scene pair (similar to the above example) is processed. For each word w and semantic feature f in the input pair, an alignment score, $a_t(w|f)$, is calculated that specifies how strongly the w–f pair are associated at time t. The alignment score in FAS10 uses the meaning probabilities of all the words in the utterance, which reflect the knowledge of the model of word meanings up to that point, as in:

$$a_t(w|f) = \frac{p_{t-1}(f|w)}{\sum\limits_{w' \in U_t} p_{t-1}(f|w')} \tag{1}$$

where $p_{t-1}(f|w)$ is the probability of f being part of the meaning of word w at time $t-1$.

In the FAS10 model, $p_t(.|w)$ is then updated for all the words in the utterance, using the accumulated evidence from all prior and current co-occurrences of w–f pairs. Specifically, an association score is defined between a word and a feature, $\text{assoc}_t(w,f)$, which is a summation of all the alignments for that w and f up to time t.[1] This association score is then normalized using a smoothed version of the follow-

[1] In FAS10, $\text{assoc}_t(w,f) = \text{assoc}_{t-1}(w,f) + a_t(w|f)$.

ing to yield $p_t(f|w)$:

$$p_t(f|w) = \frac{\text{assoc}_t(f, w)}{\sum\limits_{f' \in \mathcal{M}} \text{assoc}_t(f', w)} \quad (2)$$

where $\mathcal{M}$ is the set of all observed features.

There are two observations to make about the FAS10 model in the context of our desire to explore attention and forgetting mechanisms in word learning. First, the calculation of alignments $a_t(w|f)$ in Eqn. (1) treats all words equally, without special attention to any particular item(s) in the input. Second, the $\text{assoc}_t(f,w)$ term in Eqn. (2) encodes perfect memory of all calculated alignments since it is a simple accumulated sum. These properties motivate the changes to the formulation of the model that we describe next.

2.2 Adding Attention to Novelty to the Model

As noted just above, the FAS10 model lacks any mechanism to focus attention on certain words, as is suggested by theories on the spacing effect (Hintzman, 1974). One robust observation in studies on attention is that people attend to new items in a learning scenario more than other items, leading to improved learning of the novel items (*e.g.*, Snyder et al., 2008; MacPherson and Moore, 2010; Horst et al., 2011). We thus model the effect of attention to novelty when calculating alignments in our new model: attention to a more novel word increases the strength of its alignment with a feature — and consequently the learned word–feature association — compared to the alignment of a less novel word.

We modify the original alignment formulation of FAS10 to incorporate a multiplicative novelty term as follows (cf. Eqn. (1)):

$$a_t(w,f) = \frac{p_t(f|w)}{\sum\limits_{w' \in \text{U}_t} p_t(f|w')} * \text{novelty}_t(w) \quad (3)$$

where $\text{novelty}_t(w)$ specifies the degree of novelty of a word as a simple inverse function of recency. That is, we assume that the more recently a word has been observed by the model, the less novel it appears to the model. Given a word w at time t that was last observed at time t_{last_w}, we calculate $\text{novelty}_t(w)$ as:

$$\text{novelty}_t(w) = 1 - \text{recency}(t, t_{last_w}) \quad (4)$$

where $\text{recency}(t, t_{last_w})$ is inversely proportional to the difference between t and t_{last_w}. We set $\text{novelty}(w)$ to be 1 for the first exposure of the word.

2.3 Adding a Forgetting Mechanism to the Model

Given the observation above (see end of Section 2.1) that $\text{assoc}_t(w,f)$ embeds perfect memory in the FAS10 model, we add a forgetting mechanism by reformulating $\text{assoc}_t(w,f)$ to incorporate a decay over time of the component alignments $a_t(w|f)$. In order to take a cognitively plausible approach to calculating this function, we observe that $\text{assoc}_t(w,f)$ in FAS10 serves a similar function to *activation* in the ACT-R model of memory (Anderson and Lebiere, 1998). In ACT-R, activation of an item is the sum of individual memory strengthenings for that item, just as $\text{assoc}_t(w,f)$ is a sum of individual alignment strengths for the pair (w,f). A crucial difference is that memory strengthenings in ACT-R undergo decay. Specifically, activation of an item m after t presentations is calculated as: $act(m)_t = \ln(\sum_{t'=1}^{t} 1/(t-t')^d)$, where t' is the time of each presentation, and d is a constant decay parameter.

We adapt this formulation for $\text{assoc}_t(w,f)$ with the following changes: First, in the *act* formula, the constant 1 in the numerator is the basic strength of each presentation to memory. In our model, this is not a constant but rather the strength of alignment, $a_t(w|f)$. Second, we assume that stronger alignments should be more entrenched in memory and thus decay more slowly than weaker alignments. Thus, each alignment undergoes a decay which is dependent on the strength of the alignment rather than a constant decay d. We thus define $\text{assoc}_t(w,f)$ to be:

$$assoc_t(f,w) = \ln\left(\sum_{t'=1}^{t} \frac{a_{t'}(w|f)}{(t-t')^{d_{a_{t'}}}}\right) \quad (5)$$

where the decay for each alignment $d_{a_{t'}}$ is:

$$d_{a_{t'}} = \frac{d}{a_{t'}(w|f)} \quad (6)$$

where d is a constant parameter. Note that the $d_{a_{t'}}$ decreases as $\text{a}_{t'}(w|f)$ increases.

apple: { FOOD:1, SOLID:.72, PRODUCE:.63, EDIBLE-FRUIT:.32, PLANT-PART:.22, PHYSICAL-ENTITY:.17, WHOLE:.06, $\cdots$ }

Figure 1: True meaning features & scores for *apple*.

3 Input Generation

The input data consists of a set of utterances paired with their corresponding scene representations. The utterances are taken from the child-directed speech (CDS) portion of the Manchester corpus (Theakston et al., 2001), from CHILDES (MacWhinney, 2000), which includes transcripts of conversations with 12 British children, ages 1;8 to 3;0. Every utterance is considered as a bag of lemmatized words. Half of the data is used as the development set, and the other half in the final experiments.

Because no manually-annotated semantic representation is available for any such large corpus of CDS, we use the approach of Nematzadeh et al. (2012) to generate scene representations. For each utterance a scene representation is generated artificially, by first creating an input-generation lexicon that contains the *true meaning* ($t(w)$) of all the words (w) in our corpus. The true meaning is a vector of semantic features and their assigned scores (Figure 1). The semantic features for a word, depending on its part of speech, are chosen from different sources such as WordNet.[2] The score of each feature is calculated automatically to give a higher value to the more specific features (such as FRUIT for *apple*), rather than more general features (like PHYSICAL-ENTITY for *apple*).

To generate the scene representation S of an utterance U, we probabilistically sample a subset of features from the features in $t(w)$ for each word $w \in$ U. Thus, in each occurrence of w some of its features are missing from the scene, resulting in an imperfect sampling. This imperfect sampling allows us to simulate noise and uncertainty in the input, as well as the uncertainty of a child in determining the relevant meaning elements in a scene. The scene S is the union of all the features sampled for all the words in the utterance. We note that the input-generation lexicon is only used in creating input corpora that are naturalistic (based on child-directed speech), and not in the learning of the model.

[2]http://wordnet.princeton.edu

4 Experiments

First, we examine the overall word learning behaviour in our new model. Then we look at spacing effects in the learning of novel words. In both these experiments, we compare the behavior of our model with the model of FAS10 to clearly illustrate the effects of forgetting and attention to novelty in the new model. Next we turn to further experiments exploring in more detail the interaction of forgetting and attention to novelty in producing spacing effects.

4.1 Word Learning over Time

Generally, the model of FAS10 has increasing comprehension of words as it is exposed to more input over time. In our model, we expect attention to novelty to facilitate word learning, by focusing more on newly observed words, whereas forgetting is expected to hinder learning. We need to see if the new model is able to learn words effectively when subject to the combined effects of these two influences.

To measure how well a word w is learned in each model, we compare its learned meaning $l(w)$ (a vector holding the values of the meaning probability $p(.|w)$) to its true meaning $t(w)$ (see Section 3):

$$\mathrm{acq}(w) = \mathrm{sim}(l(w), t(w)) \qquad (7)$$

where sim is the cosine similarity between the two meaning vectors, $t(w)$ and $l(w)$. The better the model learns the meaning of w, the closer $l(w)$ would get to $t(w)$, and the higher the value of sim would become. To evaluate the overall behaviour of a model, at each point in time, we average the acq score of all the words that the model has seen.

We train each model on $10,000$ input utterance–scene pairs and compare their patterns of word learning over time (Figure 2).[3] We can see that in the original model, the average acq score is mostly increasing over time before leveling off. Our model, starts at a higher average acq score compared to FAS10's model, since the effect of attention to novelty is stronger than the effect of forgetting in early stages of training. There is a sharp decrease in the acq scores after the early training stage, which then levels off. The early decrease in acq scores occurs because many of the words the model is ex-

[3]The constant decay parameter d in Eqn. (6) is set to 0.03 in this experiment.

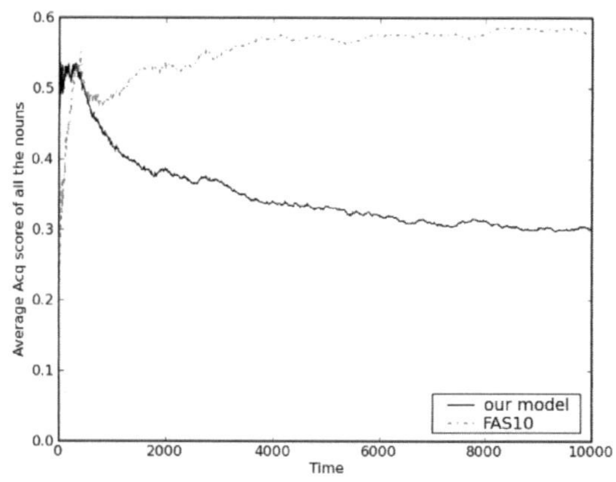

Figure 2: Average acq score of the words over time, for our model and FAS10's model.

posed to early on are not learned very well initially, and so forgetting occurs at a higher rate during that stage. The model subsequently stabilizes, and the acq scores level off although at a lower absolute level than the FAS10 model. Note that when comparing these two models, we are interested in the pattern of learning; in particular, we need to ensure that our new word learning model will eventually stabilize as expected. Our model stabilizes at a lower average acq score since unlike FAS10's model, it does not implement a perfect memory.

4.2 The Spacing Effect in Novel Word Learning

Vlach et al. (2008) performed an experiment to investigate the effect of presentation spacing in learning novel word–object pairs in three-year-old children. Each pair was presented 3 times in each of two settings, either consecutively (massed presentation), or with a short play interval between each presentation (spaced presentation). Children were then asked to identify the correct object corresponding to the novel word. The number of correct responses was significantly higher when the pairs were in the spaced presentation compared to the massed presentation. This result clearly demonstrates the spacing effect in novel word learning in children.

Experiments on the spacing effect in adults have typically examined and compared different amounts of time between the spaced presentations, which we refer to as the spacing interval. Another important parameter in such studies is the time period between the last training trial and the test trial(s), which we refer to as the retention interval (Glenberg, 1976; Bahrick and Phelps, 1987; Pavlik and Anderson, 2005). Since the experiment of Vlach et al. (2008) was designed for very young children, the procedures were kept simple and did not vary these two parameters. We design an experiment similar to that of Vlach et al. (2008) to examine the effect of spacing in our model, but extend it to also study the role of various spacing and retention intervals, for comparison to earlier adult studies.

4.2.1 Experimental Setup

First, the model is trained on 100 utterance–scene pairs to simulate the operation of normal word learning prior to the experiment.[4] Then a randomly picked novel word (*nw*) that did not appear in the training trials is introduced to the model in 3 teaching trials, similar to Vlach et al.'s (2008) experiment. For each teaching trial, *nw* is added to a different utterance, and its probabilistically-generated meaning representation (see Section 3) is added to the corresponding scene. We add *nw* to an utterance–scene pair from our corpus to simulate the presentation of the novel word during the natural interaction with the child in the experimental setting.

The spacing interval between each of these 3 teaching trials is varied from 0 to 29 utterances, resulting in 30 different simulations for each *nw*. For example, when the spacing interval is 5, there are 5 utterances between each presentation of *nw*. A spacing of 0 utterances yields the massed presentation. We run the experiment for 20 randomly-chosen novel words to ensure that the pattern of the results is not related to the meaning representation of a specific word.

For each spacing interval, we look at the acq score of the novel word at two points in time, to simulate two retention intervals: One immediately after the last presentation of the novel word (*imm* condition) and one at a later point in time (*lat* condition). By looking at these two conditions, we can further observe the effect of forgetting in our model, since the decay in the model's memory would be more severe in the *lat* condition, compared to the *imm* condition.[5] The results reported here for each spacing

[4]In the experiments of Section 4.2.2 and Section 4.3, the constant decay parameter d is equal to 0.04.

[5]Recall that each point of time in our model corresponds to

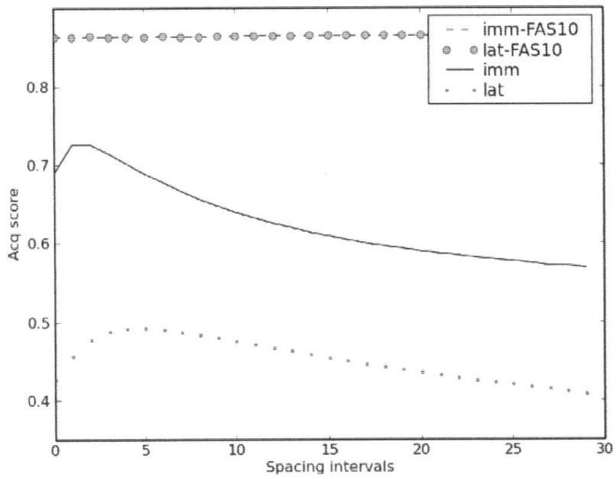

Figure 3: Average acq score of novel words over spacing intervals, in our model and FAS10's model.

interval average the acq scores of all the novel words at the corresponding points in time.

4.2.2 The Basic Spacing Effect Results

Figure 3 shows the results of the simulations in our model and the FAS10 model. We assume that very small spacing intervals (but greater than 0) correspond to the spaced presentation in the Vlach et al. (2008) experiments, while a spacing of 0 corresponds to the massed presentation. In the FAS10 model, the average acq score of words does not change with spacing, and there is no difference between the *imm* and *lat* conditions, confirming that this model fails to mimic the observed spacing effects. By contrast, in our model the average acq score is greater in the small spacing intervals (1-3) than in the massed presentation, mimicking the Vlach et al. (2008) results on children. This happens because a *nw* appears more novel with larger spacing intervals between each of its presentations resulting in stronger alignments.

We can see two other interesting patterns in our model: First, the average acq score of words for all spacing intervals is greater in the *imm* condition than in the *lat* condition. This occurs because there is more forgetting in the model over the longer retention interval of *lat*. Second, in both conditions the average acq score initially increases from a massed presentation to the smaller spacing intervals. However, at spacing intervals between about 3 and 5, the acq score begins to decrease as spacing intervals grow larger. As explained earlier, the initial increase in acq scores for small spacing intervals results from novelty of the words in a spaced presentation. However, for bigger spacing intervals the effect of novelty is swamped by the much greater degree of forgetting after a bigger spacing interval.

Although Vlach et al. (2008) did not vary their spacing and retention intervals, other spacing effect studies on adults have done so. For example, Glenberg (1976) presented adults with word pairs to learn under varying spacing intervals, and tested them after several different retention intervals (his experiment 1). Our pattern of results in Figure 3 is in line with his results. In particular, he found a nonmonotonic pattern of spacing similar to the pattern in our model: learning of pairs was improved with increasing spacing intervals up to a point, but there was a decrease in performance for larger spacing intervals. Also, the proportion of recalled pairs decreased for longer retention intervals, similar to our lower performance in the *lat* condition.

4.3 The Role of Forgetting and Attention

To fully understand the role as well as the necessity of, both forgetting and attention to novelty in our results, we test two other models under the same conditions as the previous spacing experiment: (a) a model with our mechanism for attention to novelty but not forgetting, and (b) a model with our forgetting mechanism but no attention to novelty; see Figure 4 and Figure 5, respectively.

In the model that attends to novelty but does not incorporate a memory decay mechanism (Figure 4), the average acq score consistently increases as spacing intervals grow bigger. This occurs because the novel words appear more novel following bigger spacing intervals, and thus attract more alignment strength. Since the model does not forget, there is no difference between the immediate (*imm*) and later (*lat*) retention intervals. This pattern does not match the spacing effect patterns of people, suggesting that forgetting is a necessary aspect of our model's ability to do so in the previous section.

On the other hand, in the model with forgetting but no attentional mechanism (Figure 5), we see two different behaviors in the *imm* and *lat* conditions. In the *imm* condition, the average acq score decreases

processing an input pair. The acq score in the *imm* condition is calculated at time t, which is immediately after the last presentation of *nw*. The *lat* condition corresponds to $t+20$.

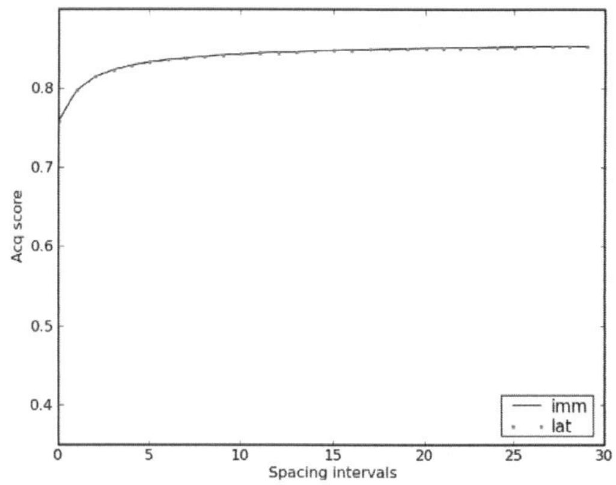

Figure 4: Average acq score of the novel words over spacing intervals, for the model with novelty but without forgetting.

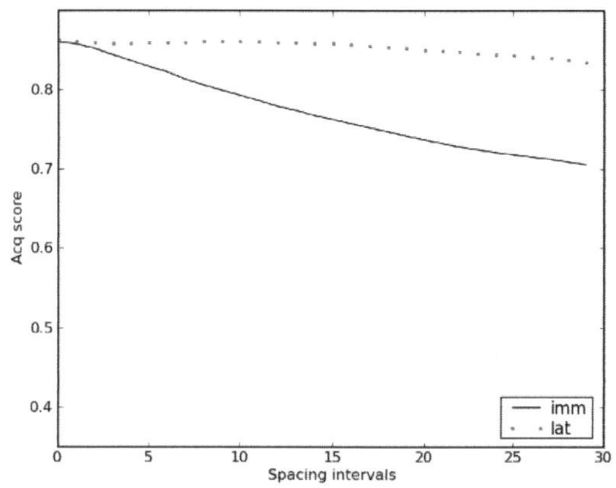

Figure 5: Average acq score of the novel words over spacing intervals, for the model with forgetting but without novelty.

consistently over spacing intervals. This is as expected, because the greater time between presentations means a greater degree of forgetting. Specifically, the alignment scores decay more between presentations of the word to be learned, given the greater passage of time in larger spacing intervals. The weaker alignments then lead to lower acq scores in this condition.

Paradoxically, although this effect on learning also holds in the *lat* condition, another factor is at play, leading to better performance than in the *imm* condition at all spacing intervals. Here the greater retention interval — the time between the last learning presentation and the test time — leads to greater forgetting in a manner that instead improves the acq scores. Consider that the meaning representation for a word includes some probability mass assigned to irrelevant features — i.e., those features that occurred in an utterance–scene pair with the word but are not part of its true meaning. Because such features generally have lower probability than relevant features (which are observed more consistently with a word), a longer retention interval leads to them decaying more than the relevant features. Thus the *lat* condition enables the model to better focus on the features relevant to a word.

In conclusion, neither attention to novelty nor forgetting alone achieves the pattern typical of the spacing effects in people that our model shows in the lower two plots in Figure 3. Hence we conclude that both factors are necessary to our account, suggesting that it is an interaction between the two that accounts for people's behaviour.

4.4 The "Spacing Crossover Interaction"

In our model with attention to novelty and forgetting (see Section 4.2), the average acq score was always better in the *imm* condition than the *lat* condition. However, researchers have observed other patterns in spacing experiments. A particularly interesting pattern found in some studies is that the plots of the results for earlier and later retention intervals cross as the spacing intervals are increased. That is, with smaller spacing intervals, a shorter retention interval (such as our *imm* condition) leads to better results, but with larger spacing intervals, a longer retention interval (such as our *lat* condition) leads to better results (Bahrick, 1979; Pavlik and Anderson, 2005). This interaction of spacing and retention intervals results in a pattern referred to as the spacing crossover interaction (Pavlik and Anderson, 2005). This pattern is different from Glenberg's (1976) experiment and from the pattern of results shown earlier for our model (Figure 3).

We looked at an experiment in which the spacing crossover pattern was observed: Pavlik and Anderson (2005) taught Japanese–English pairs to subjects, varying the spacing and retention intervals. One difference we noticed between the experiment of Pavlik and Anderson (2005) and Glenberg (1976) was that in the former, the presentation period of the stimulus was 5 seconds, whereas in the latter, it was 3 seconds. We hypothesize that the difference between the amount of time for the presentation peri-

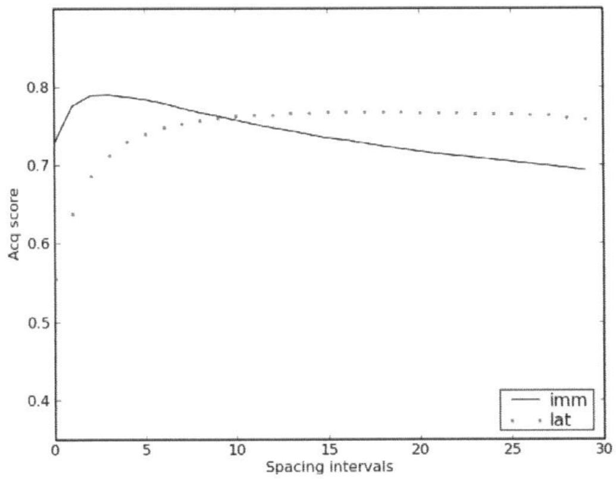

Figure 6: Average acq score of the novel words over spacing intervals

ods might explain the different spacing patterns in these experiments.

We currently cannot model presentation time directly in our model, since having access to an input longer does not change its computation of alignments between words and features. However, we can indirectly model a difference in presentation time by modifying the amount of memory decay: We assume that when an item is presented longer, it is learned better and therefore subject to less forgetting. We run the spacing experiment with a smaller forgetting parameter to model the longer presentation period used in Pavlik and Anderson's (2005) versus Glenberg (1976).[6]

Our results using the decreased level of forgetting, given in Figure 6, show the expected crossover interaction between the retention and spacing intervals: for smaller spacing intervals, the acq scores are better in the *imm* condition, whereas for larger spacing intervals, they are better in the *lat* condition. Thus, our model suggests an explanation for the observed crossover: in tasks which strengthen the learning of the target item — and thus lessen the effect of forgetting — we expect to see a benefit of later retention trials in experiments with people.

5 General Discussion and Future Work

The spacing effect (where people learn items better when multiple presentations are spread over time) has been studied extensively and is found to be robust over different types of tasks and domains. Many experiments have examined the spacing effect in the context of word learning and other similar tasks. Particularly, in a recent study of Vlach et al. (2008), young children demonstrated a spacing effect in a novel word learning task.

We use computational modeling to show that by changing a probabilistic associative model of word learning to include both a forgetting and attentional mechanism, the new model can account not only for the child data, but for various patterns of spacing effect data in adults. Specifically, our model shows the nonmonotonic pattern of spacing observed in the experimental data, where learning improves in shorter spacing intervals, but worsens in bigger spacing intervals. Our model can also replicate the observed cross-over interaction between spacing and retention intervals: for smaller spacing intervals, performance is better when tested after a shorter retention interval, whereas for bigger spacing intervals, it is better after longer retention intervals. Finally, our results confirm that by modelling word learning as a standalone development process, we cannot account for the spacing effect. Instead, it is important to consider word learning in the context of fundamental cognitive processes of memory and attention.

Much remains to be investigated in our model. For example, most human experiments examine the effect of frequency of presentations of target items. Also, the range of retention intervals that has been studied is greater than what we have considered here. In the future, we plan to study the effect of these two parameters. In addition, with our current model, the amount of time an item is presented to the learner does not play a role. We can also reformulate our alignment mechanism to incorporate a notion of the amount of time to consider an item to be learned. Another interesting future direction, especially in the context of word learning, is to develop a more complete attentional mechanism, that considers different parameters such as social cues and linguistic cues. Finally, we will study the role of forgetting and attention in modelling other relevant experimental data (*e.g.*, Kachergis et al., 2009; Vlach and Sandhofer, 2010).

[6]Here, the decay parameter is set to 0.03.

References

John .R. Anderson and Christian Lebiere. 1998. *The atomic components of thought.* Lawrence Erlbaum Associates.

Harry P. Bahrick. 1979. Maintenance of knowledge: Questions about memory we forgot to ask. *Journal of Experimental Psychology: General*, 108(3):296–308.

Harry P. Bahrick and Elizabeth Phelps. 1987. Retention of Spanish vocabulary over 8 years. *Journal of Experimental Psychology: Learning, Memory, and Cognition*, 13(2):344–349.

Paul Bloom. 2000. *How Children Learn the Meanings of Words.* MIT Press.

Susan Carey. 1978. The child as word learner. In M. Halle, J. Bresnan, and G. A. Miller, editors, *Linguistic Theory and Psychological Reality*. The MIT Press.

Malinda Carpenter, Katherine Nagell, Michael Tomasello, George Butterworth, and Chris Moore. 1998. Social cognition, joint attention, and communicative competence from 9 to 15 months of age. *Monographs of the Society for Research in Child Development, 63(4).*

Nicholas J. Cepeda, Harold Pashler, Edward Vul, John T. Wixted, and Doug Rohrer. 2006. Distributed practice in verbal recall tasks: A review and quantitative synthesis. *Psychological Bulletin*, 132(3):354 – 380.

Lauren J. Cuddy and Larry L. Jacoby. 1982. When forgetting helps memory: an analysis of repetition effects. *Journal of Verbal Learning and Verbal Behavior*, 21(4):451 – 467.

Frank Dempster. 1989. Spacing effects and their implications for theory and practice. *Educational Psychology Review*, 1:309–330.

Frank N. Dempster. 1996. Distributing and managing the conditions of encoding and practice. *Memory*, pages 317–344.

Hermann Ebbinghaus. 1885. *Memory: A contribution to experimental psychology.* New York, Teachers College, Columbia University.

Afsaneh Fazly, Afra Alishahi, and Suzanne Stevenson. 2010. A probabilistic computational model of cross-situational word learning. *Cognitive Science*, 34(6):1017–1063.

Michael C. Frank, Sharon Goldwater, Thomas L. Griffiths, and Joshua B. Tenenbaum. 2010. Modeling human performance in statistical word segmenation. *Cognition*, 117:107–125.

Arthur Glenberg. 1979. Component-levels theory of the effects of spacing of repetitions on recall and recognition. *Memory and Cognition*, 7:95–112.

Arthur M. Glenberg. 1976. Monotonic and nonmonotonic lag effects in paired-associate and recognition memory paradigms. *Journal of Verbal Learning & Verbal Behavior*, 15(1).

Roberta M. Golinkoff, Kathy Hirsh-Pasek, Leslie M. Bailey, and Neil R. Wegner. 1992. Young children and adults use lexical principles to learn new nouns. *Developmental Psychology*, 28(1):99–108.

Douglas L. Hintzman. 1974. Theoretical implications of the spacing effect.

Jessica S. Horst, Larissa K. Samuelson, Sarah C. Kucker, and Bob McMurray. 2011. Whats new? children prefer novelty in referent selection. *Cognition*, 118(2):234 – 244.

Larry L. Jacoby. 1978. On interpreting the effects of repetition: Solving a problem versus remembering a solution. *Journal of Verbal Learning and Verbal Behavior*, 17(6):649 – 667.

George Kachergis, Chen Yu, and Richard Shiffrin. 2009. Temporal contiguity in cross-situational statistical learning.

Amy C. MacPherson and Chris Moore. 2010. Understanding interest in the second year of life. *Infancy*, 15(3):324–335.

Brian MacWhinney. 2000. *The CHILDES Project: Tools for Analyzing Talk*, volume 2: The Database. Erlbaum, 3rd edition.

Ellen M. Markman and Gwyn F. Wachtel. 1988. Children's use of mutual exclusivity to constrain the meanings of words. *Cognitive Psychology*, 20:121–157.

Arthur W. Melton. 1967. Repetition and retrieval from memory. *Science*, 158:532.

Aida Nematzadeh, Afsaneh Fazly, and Suzanne Stevenson. 2012. Interaction of word learning and semantic category formation in late talking. In *Proc. of CogSci'12*. To appear.

Philip I. Pavlik and John R. Anderson. 2005. Practice and forgetting effects on vocabulary memory: An activationbased model of the spacing effect. *Cognitive Science*, 29:559–586.

W.V.O. Quine. 1960. *Word and Object*. MIT Press.

Terry Regier. 2005. The emergence of words: Attentional learning in form and meaning. *Cognitive Science*, 29:819–865.

Jeffery Mark Siskind. 1996. A computational study of cross-situational techniques for learning word-to-meaning mappings. *Cognition*, 61:39–91.

Linda B Smith, Eliana Colunga, and Hanako Yoshida. 2010. Knowledge as process: Contextually-cued attention and early word learning. *Cogn Sci*, 34(7):1287–314.

Kelly A. Snyder, Michael P. BlanK, and chad J. Marsolek. 2008. What form of memory underlies novelty preferences? *Psychological Bulletin and Review*, 15(2):315 – 321.

Anna L. Theakston, Elena V. Lieven, Julian M. Pine, and Caroline F. Rowland. 2001. The role of performance limitations in the acquisition of verb–argument structure: An alternative account. *J. of Child Language*, 28:127–152.

Haley A Vlach and Catherine M Sandhofer. 2010. Desirable difficulties in cross-situational word learning.

Haley A. Vlach, Catherine M. Sandhofer, and Nate Kornell. 2008. The Spacing Effect in Children's Memory and Category Induction. *Cognition*, 109(1):163–167, October.

Chen Yu. 2005. The emergence of links between lexical acquisition and object categorization: A computational study. *Connection Science*, 17(3–4):381–397.

Author Index